John Howard

Extracts Selected from the Writings and Observations of the Late John Howard

The State of Prisons and Hospitals in Holland, Germany, Italy, Geneva, Switzerland,

Austrian Flanders, French Flanders and France

John Howard

Extracts Selected from the Writings and Observations of the Late John Howard
The State of Prisons and Hospitals in Holland, Germany, Italy, Geneva, Switzerland, Austrian Flanders, French Flanders and France

ISBN/EAN: 9783337126759

Printed in Europe, USA, Canada, Australia, Japan

Cover: Foto ©Andreas Hilbeck / pixelio.de

More available books at **www.hansebooks.com**

EXTRACTS

SELECTED fiom the

Writings and Observations

OF THE LATE

JOHN HOWARD, ESQ.

LL.D. and F.R.S.

VIZ.

THE STATE OF PRISONS AND HOSPITALS

In Holland, Germany, Italy, Geneva, Switzerland, Auſtrian Flanders, French Flanders, and France; Scotland and Ireland:

With a Particular Account of the Engliſh Priſons,

IN

London; and County Gaols at Hartfordſhire, Eſſex, Kent, Suſſex, Surry, Buckinghamſhire, Bedfordſhire, Huntingdonſhire, Cambridgeſhire, Norfold, Suffold, Warwickſhire, Leiceſterſhire, Derbyſhire, Nottinghamſhire, Lincolnſhire, Northamptonſhire, Berkſhire, Oxfordſhire, Worceſterſhire, Staffordſhire, Shropſhire, Herefordſhire. Monmouthſhire. Glouceſterſhire, Hampſhire, Wiltſhire, Dorfetſhire, Devonſhire, Cornwell, Somerſetſhire, Yorkſhire, Durham, Newcaſtle, Northumberland, Cumberland, Weſtmorland, Lancaſhire, Cheſhire, &c.

TO WHICH IS ADDED, AN

A C C O U N T

OF THE

L A Z A R E T T O E S.

NEWCASTLE:

PRINTED BY W. THOMPSON.

M,DCC,XC.

ADDRESS.

THE recent death of Mr HOWARD having turned the attention of the public in a wonderful degree to the purfuits of their common Benefactor, little apology will be needed for giving to the world fome account of that great man. All that may be neceffary on the prefent occafion, is to advance that no pains have been fpared to collect materials, and obtain the moft authentic intelligence.

In order to aid the general object of his benevolence, it was the cuftom of Mr Howard to give away, a great many copies of his different productions. This, of courfe, narrowed the number on fale, and thro' the lapfe of time and the great avidity with which they have been bought up, his works are now not to be had, at any price. The editor has therefore added fome extracts from his more valuable productions, which he trufts will be favourably received. And he cannot omit this opportunity of adding, that nothing can be more congenial to the fpirit of their benign author, than an exertion to diffeminate, in the moft general manner, the wretchednefs, the difeafe and the enormities which difgrace our prifons and hofpitals; together with the falutary regulations which have, and may be applied to thefe manfions of mifery.

S T A T E of P R I S O N S.

Ah little think the gay·····················
Whom pleafure, power, and affluence furround,
How many pine in want, and dungeon-glooms;
Shut from the common air.

THOMSON.

GENERAL VIEW of DISTRESS
in PRISONS.

THERE are prifons, into which, whoever looks will, at the firft fight of the people confined there, be convinced that there is fome great error in the management of them: The fallow, meagre countenances declare, without words, that they are very miferable. Many who went in healthy, are in a few months changed into emaciated, dejected objects. Some are feen pining under difeafes, "*fick, and in prifon;*" expiring on the floors, in loathfome cells, of peftilential fevers and the confluent fmall pox: Victims—I will not fay to the cruelty, but I muft fay to the inattention of fheriffs, and gentlemen in the commiffion of the peace.

The caufe of this diftrefs is, that many prifons are fcantily fupplied, and fome, almoft totally unprovided with the neceffaries of life.

There are feveral *Bridewells* in which the prifoners have no allowance of *food* at all. In fome, the keeper farms

A   what

what little is allowed them: And where he engages to supply each prifoner with one or two penny-worth of bread a-day, I have known this fhrunk to half, fometimes *lefs* than half the quantity, cut or broken from his own loaf.

It will perhaps be afked, does not their work maintain them? for every one knows that thofe offenders are committed to *hard labour*. The anfwer to that queftion, tho' true, will hardly be believed. There are very few Bridewells, in which any work is done, or can be done. The prifoners have neither tools nor materials of any kind; but fpend their time in floth, profanenefs and debauchery, in a degree, which in fome of thofe houfes that I have feen is extremely fhocking.

Some keepers of thefe houfes, who have reprefented to the magiftrates the wants of their prifoners, and defired for them neceffary food, have been filenced with thefe inconfiderate words, *Let them work or flarve*. When thofe gentlemen know the former is impoffible, do they not by that fentence, inevitably doom poor creatures to the latter?

I have afked fome keepers, fince the late act for preferving the health of prifoners, why no care is taken of their fick: And have been anfwered, that the magiftrates tell them, *the act does not extend to Bridewells*.

In confequence of this, you fee prifoners at the quarter feffions, covered (hardly covered) with rags; almoft famifhed; and fick of difeafes, which the difcharged fpread wherever they go, and with which thofe who are fent to the county gaols, infect thefe prifoners.

The fame complaint *(want of food)* is to be found in many *County gaols*. In about half thefe, debtors have no bread;

bread; altho' it is granted to the highwayman, the houfe-breaker, and the murderer; and medical affiftance, which is provided for the latter, is witheld from the former. In many of thefe gaols, debtors who would work are not permitted to have any tools, left they fhould furnifh felons with them for efcape or other mifchief. I have often feen thefe prifoners eating their water-foup (bread boiled in mere water) and heard them fay—" We are locked up and almoft ftarved to death."

Felons have in fome gaols two penny-worth of bread a-day; in fome three halfpenny worth; in fome a penny-worth; in fome none. It is not uncommon to fee the whole purchafe, efpecially of the fmaller fums, eaten at breakfaft; which is fometimes the cafe when they receive their pittance but once in two days: And then on the following day they muft faft.

This allowance being fo far fhort of the cravings of nature, and in fome prifons leffened by farming to the gaoler, many criminals are half ftarved: Such of them as at their commitment were in health, come out almoft famifhed, fcarce able to move, and for weeks incapable of any labour.

Many prifons have *no water*. This defect is frequent in Bridewells and Town gaols. In the felons' court in fome County gaols there is no water: In fome places where there is water, prifoners are always locked up within doors, and have no more than the keeper or his fervants think fit to bring them: In one place, they were limited to three pints a-day each—a fcanty provifion for drink and cleanli-nefs!

And as to air which is no lefs neceffary than the two preceding articles, and given us by Providence quite *gratis*,

without

without any care or labour of our own; yet as if the boun-
teous goodnefs of Heaven excited our envy, methods are
contrived to rob prifoners of this *genuine cordial of life*, as
Dr Hales very properly calls it : I mean by preventing that
circulation and change of the falutiferous fluid, without
which animals cannot live and thrive. It is well known
that air which has performed its office in the lungs, is fe-
culent and noxious. Writers upon the fubject fhew, that
a hogfhead of it, will laft a man only an hour: But thofe
who do not chufe to confult philofophers, may judge from
a notorious fact. In 1756, at Calcutta in Bengal, out of
170 perfons who were confined in a hole there, one night
150 were taken out dead. The few furvivors afcribed their
mortality to the want of frefh air, and called the place, from
what they had fuffered there, *Hell in miniature!*

Air which has been breathed, is made poifonous to a
more intenfe degree, by the effluvia from the fick, and what
elfe in prifons is offenfive. My reader will judge of its
malignity when I affure him, that my cloths were, in my
firft journeys, fo offenfive, that in a poft chaife I could not
bear the windows drawn up; and was therefore often
obliged to travel on horfeback. The leaves of my memo-
randum-book were often fo tainted, that I could not ufe it 'till
after fpreading it an hour or two before the fire : And even
my antidote, a vial of vinegar, has, after ufing it in a few
prifons, become intollerably difagreeable. I did not wonder that in thofe journeys, many gaolers made excufes; and
did not go with me into the felons' wards.

From hence any one may judge of the probability, there
is againft the health and life of prifoners, crowded in clofe
rooms, cells and fubterraneous dungeons, for fourteen or
fixteen hours out of the four-and-twenty. In fome of thofe
caverns the floor is very damp; in others, there is fometimes

times an inch or two of water; and the ſtraw or bedding is laid upon ſuch floors, ſeldom on barrack bedſteads.

One cauſe why the rooms in ſome priſons are ſo cloſe, is perhaps the window-tax, which the gaolers have to pay: This tempts them to ſtop the windows, and ſtifle their pri- ſoners.

In many gaols and in moſt bridewells, there is no al- lowance of *bedding* or *ſtraw* for priſoners to ſleep on. And if by any means they get a little, it is not changed for months together, ſo that it is almoſt worn to duſt. Some lie upon rags, others upon the bare floors. When I have complained of this to the keepers, their juſtification has been, " The county allows no ſtraw, the priſoners have " none but at my coſt."

I am ready to think, that none who give credit to what is contained in the foregoing detail, will wonder at the ha- vock made by the *gaol fever*. From my own obſervations in 1773 and 1774, I was fully convinced that many more were deſtroyed by it, than were put to death by all the public executions in the kingdom. This frequent effect of confinement in priſons ſeems generally underſtood, and ſhews how full of emphatical meaning is the curſe of a ſe- vere creditor, who pronounces his debtor's doom to *rot in gaol*. I believe I have learned the full import of this ſen- tence, from the vaſt numbers who to my certain know- ledge, ſome of them before my eyes, have periſhed in our gaols.

But the miſchief is not confined to priſons—multitudes catch the diſtemper, by going to their relatives and ac- quaintance in the gaols: Many others from priſoners diſ- charged: And not a few in the courts of judicature.

Baker

Baker in his Chronicle, page 353, mentioning the affize held in Oxford caftle, 1577 (called, from its fatal confequence, the *black affize*) informs us that " all who were " prefent died in forty hours: The lord chief baron, the " fheriff, and about three hundred more." Lord chancellor Bacon afcribes this to a difeafe brought into court by the prifoners; and Dr Mead is of the fame opinion.

At the Lent affize in Taunton, 1730, fome prifoners who were brought thither from Ivelchefter gaol, infected the court; and lord chief baron Pengelly; Sir James Sheppard, ferjeant; John Pigot, Efq; fheriff, and fome hundreds befides, died of the *gaol diftemper*. The numbers that were carried off by the fame malady in London, in 1750, two judges, the lord mayor, one alderman, and many of inferior rank, are two well known to need the mentioning further particulars.

It were eafy to multiply inftances of this mifchief; but thofe which have been mentioned are, I prefume, fufficient to fhew, even if no mercy were due to prifoners, that the gaol diftemper is a national concern of no fmall importance.

BAD CUSTOMS in PRISONS.

A cruel cuftom obtains in moft of our gaols, which is that of the prifoners demanding of a new comer, *garnifh*, *footing*, or (as it is called in fome London gaols) *chummage*. " Pay or ftrip," are the fatal words. I fay, *fatal;* for fo they are to fome; who having no money, are obliged to give up part of their fcanty apparel; and if they have no bedding or ftraw to fleep on, contract difeafes, which I have known to prove mortal.

Gaming,

Gaming, in various forms is very frequent: Cards, dice, ſkittles, Miſſiſippi and Porto-bello tables, billiards, fives, tennis, &c. In the country the three firſt are moſt common; and eſpecially cards. There is ſcarce a county gaol but is furniſhed with them: And one can ſeldom go in without ſeeing priſoners at play. I am not an enemy to diverting exerciſe: Yet the riot, brawling, and profaneneſs, that are the uſual conſequences of their play; the circumſtances of debtors gaming away the property of their creditors, which has been done to a conſiderable amount; hindering their fellow-priſoners, who do not play, from walking in the courts, while they do; of which inconvenience I have heard them complain: Theſe ſeem to me cogent reaſons for prohibiting all kinds of gaming within the walls of a priſon.

Loading priſoners with *heavy irons*, which make their walking and even lying down to ſleep, difficult and painful, is another cuſtom which I cannot but condemn. In ſome county gaols the *women* do not eſcape this ſeverity: But in London they do: And therefore it is not neceſſary in the country. The practice muſt be mere tyranny; unleſs it proceed from avarice; which I rather ſuſpect; becauſe county gaolers do ſometimes grant diſpenſations, and indulge their priſoners, men as well as women, with what they call the " *choice of irons*," if they will pay for it.

Gaol delivery is in ſome counties *but once a year:* What reparation can be made to a poor creature for the miſery he has ſuffered by confinement in priſon near twelve months before a trial, in which perhaps, he is declared by his country *not guilty?*

One cauſe of gaol delivery being ſo ſeldom, is, *in ſome places*, the expence of entertaining the judges and their retinue.

nue.   At Hull they ufed to have the affize but once in feven years.   Peacock, a *murderer*, was in prifon there near
three years : Before his trial, the principal witnefs died ;
and the criminal was acquitted.   They now have it once
in three years.

Altho' acquitted prifoners are, by the late act in their
favour,* cleared of gaolers' fees ; they are ftill fubject to a
fimilar demand made by *clerks of the affize* and *clerks of
the peace*, and detained in prifon feveral days after their ac-
quittal, at affize, till the judges—at quarter feffions, till
the juftices of peace leave the town; in order to obtain
thofe fees, which the gentlemen fay are not cancelled by
the act,   And yet the exprefs words of it are, *Acquitted
prifoners* " fhall be immediately fet at large in open court."
It is evident then, that all fees of the commitment in refpect to the prifoner, are by this act totally abolifhed.

I was informed at Durham, that judge Gold, at the affize
1775. laid a *fine* of fifty pounds on the gaoler *for detaining*
fome acquitted prifoners, for the fees of the clerk of affize.
But upon the interceffion of the bifhop (proprietor of the
gaol) the fine was remitted ; and the prifoner fet at large:
The judge ordering the clerk of affize to explain to him in
London the foundation of his demand.

An ACCOUNT of FOREIGN PRISONS
and HOSPITALS.

I defigned to publifh the account of our prifons in the
fpring 1775, after I returned from Scotland and Ireland.
But

---

* 14th George III.

But conjecturing that something useful to my purpose might be collected abroad, I laid aside my papers, and travelled into France, Flanders, Holland, and Germany. I flattered myself that my labour was not quite fruitless; and repeated my visit to these countries, and went also to Switzerland, in 1776.

In the conclusion of my former edition, I made a promise, if the legislature should seriously engage in the reformation of our prisons, to take a third journey, through the Austrian and Prussian dominions, and the free cities of Germany. This I accomplished in 1778, and likewise extended my tour through Italy, and revisited some of the countries I had before seen in pursuit of my object.

The substance of all these travels is now thrown into one narrative, in which I follow the order of my last journey, and begin with

H O L L A N D.

Prisons in the *United Provinces* are so quiet, and most of them so clean, that a visitor can hardly believe he is in a gaol. They are commonly (except the rasp-houses) white washed once or twice a year: And a prisoner told me it was no small refreshment to go into their rooms after such a thorough cleaning. A physician and surgeon is appointed to every prison; and prisoners are in general healthy.

In most of the prisons for *criminals* there are so many rooms that each prisoner is kept separate. They never go out of their rooms: Each has a bedstead, straw, mat, and coverlet. But there are few criminals, except those in

B   the

the *rasp-houses* and *spin-houses*. Of late, in all the seven
provinces, seldom more executions in a year than from four
to six.   One reason of this, I believe, is the awful solem-
nity of executions, which are performed in presence of the
magistrates, with great order and seriousness, and great effect on the spectators. I did not see the process in Holland;
but it was particularly described to me, and was similar to
what I had been witness of in another place abroad.

The common method of execution for unpremeditated
murder, is decollation by the broad sword. Robberies are
generally punished by the halter.   For the more atrocious
crimes, such as premeditated murder, &c. the malefactor
is broken on the wheel; or rather on a cross laid flat upon
the scaffold.   But a description of the manner of this execution, which is finished by a *coup de grace* on the breast,
would not be agreeable to any of my readers.

Debtors also are but few.   The magistrates do not ap-
prove of confining in idleness any that may be usefully employed.   And when one is imprisoned, the creditor must
pay the gaoler for his maintenance, from five and a half
to eighteen stivers a day, according to the debtor's former
condition in life.   The aliment must be paid every week:
In default whereof, the gaoler gives eight days notice; and
if within that time, the money, or security for it, be not
brought, the debtor is discharged.

Another reason is, that the situation is very disgraceful.
But perhaps the principal cause that debtors, as well as capital offenders, are few, is the great care that is taken to
train up the children of the poor, and indeed of all others,
to industry.   No debtors have their wives and children
living with them in prison: But occasional visits in the day-
time are not forbidden.   You do not hear in the streets as

you

you pafs by a prifon, what I have been rallied for abroad, the cry of *poor hungry ſtarving debtors.*

The States do not tranſport convicts: But men are put to labour in the *raſp-houſes*, and women to proper work in the *ſpin-houſes:* Upon this profeſſed maxim, *Make them diligent. and they will be honeſt.* The raſping logwood, which was formerly the principal work done by the male convicts, is now in many places performed at the mills, much cheaper: And the Dutch, finding woollen manufactures more profitable, have lately ſet up ſeveral of them in thoſe houſes of correction. In ſome, the work of the healthy priſoners does not only ſupport them; but they have a little extra time to earn ſomewhat for their better living in priſon, or for their benefit afterwards.

Great care is taken to give them moral and religious inſtruction. and reform their manners, for their own and the public good. The *chaplain* (ſuch there is in every houſe of correction) does not only perform public worſhip, but privately inſtructs the priſoners, catechiſes them every week, &c. and I am well informed that many come out ſober and honeſt.* Some have even choſen to continue and work in the houſe after their diſcharge.

Offenders are ſentenced to theſe houſes, according to their crimes, for ſeven, ten, fifteen, twenty years and upwards; but, to prevent deſpair, ſeldom for life. As an encouragement to ſobriety and induſtry, thoſe who diſ-

B 2   tinguiſh

---

* I have heard in England that a countryman of ours, who was a priſoner in the raſp-houſe at Amſterdam ſeveral years, was permitted to work at his own trade, ſhoe-making; and by being conſtantly kept employed, was quite cured of the vices which brought him to confinement. My informant added, that the priſoner received at his releaſe a ſurplus of his earnings, which enabled him to ſet up in London; where he lived in credit, and at dinner commonly drank " Health to his worthy maſters at the raſp-houſe."

tinguifh themfelves by fuch behaviour, are difcharged before the expiration of their term.   A prifoner who gives
information of an intended efcape is favoured much in
this refpeft; his term is confiderably fhortened.   A little
before the election of new magiftrates, thofe who are in
office infpect thefe prifons, and enquire of the keeper which
prifoners, of thofe who have been confined a few years,
have been diligent and orderly; and of the minifter,
which of them have been · moft attentive to public and
private inftructions.   According to the accounts, they
abridge the appointed time of punifhment; fo that fourteen years will fometimes be reduced to eight or ten, and
twelve years to fix or feven.   This practice is in every
view wife and beneficial.   Indeed, I have fome reafon to
think that criminals are often doomed to a longer term,
with an intention to make fuch deductions upon their a-
mendment.

In Holland, as well as in Germany, there are private
rooms in moft of the houfes of correction, in which young
perfons, of a vicious and · profligate turn, are confined on
the reprefentation of their parents, till they fhew figns of
amendment.

At ROTTERDAM, in the Stadt-houfe prifon, were no
debtors in any of the three rooms at any of my vifits.   When
there are any, they are alimented at one fixed fum, viz.
fixteen ftivers a day.   There are feven rooms for criminals
or diforderly perfons.   One of them is called the *condemned* room, into which a criminal is put fourteen days before
his final fentence; and immediately after the fentence, he
is executed with a folemnity very ftriking to the common
people.   In three of the rooms, were three perfons confined, for a limited time, for fome fmall offences, and kept to
bread and water.   Their daily allowance was from four to
                                                                             five

five ſtivers, and their pitcher was filled with *water* three times a day; but the other criminals had their pitcher filled once a day with *beer*, and their allowance was from nine to ten ſtivers.* There were caſes with thick ſtraw mats, and two or three coverlets to each.

The whipping-poſt is in the middle of the court, in full view of the *men*-criminals. For the more refractory, there are dark rooms, but not dungeons: In one of theſe, on ſhutting the door on myſelf, I found no dampneſs. My conductor obſerved, that the floor was raiſed to preſerve it dry. Here they are allowed no bedding, and are kept to bread and water, which is given them at an aperture in the door. Their confinement is for ſix, eight, ten, or fourteen days.

Being at Rotterdam on a Sunday, I was deſirous of ſeeing whether there was ſuch diſſipation in their priſoners, as there is in ours, on that day. The public ſervice at the Raſp-houſe began at half after one o'clock. The audience conſiſted of about thirty or forty inhabitants of the town, Mr Schumaker, the preſiding regent, the head-keeper and his family, and three under-keepers, beſides the priſoners. The number of *women* priſoners was about forty, who were ſeparated from the reſt of the congregation, by a wooden paliſade, and ſeated on benches raiſed one above another. They were all clean and neat; had nothing diſtinguiſhing in their dreſs, but were without hats. While they ſtood up, during prayer, they held up their aprons to cover their faces. The *men* were neat, dreſſed in brown coats, had

been

* As I was there at one o'clock, the time of the diſtribution, I obſerved that the bread was all cut in ſlices: This prevents thoſe conteſts or frauds which ſometimes happen where priſoners meſs together, and the bread is given out in one loaf, as I ſaw on board the hulks in the Thames, where one loaf was given to ſix perſons.

been fhaved, had clean fhirts (which were moft of them chequed), clean ftockings, and wore handkerchiefs about their necks.   They alfo were feated on raifed benches, in a room out of the chapel, and feparated from it by an iron grate from the top of the room to the bottom, fo wide, that all the audience, except the female prifoners, had them full in view.   The keeper's feat adjoins to this grate, and two of his fervants, who are turnkeys, fat obferving their beha-viour.

The chaplain, after a fhort prayer, preached extempore; then, the *men* convicts joined in finging, moft of them hav-ing books.   When the chaplain had prayed again, he ca-techifed for about three quarters of an hour.   It being the *womens'* turn that Sunday, fix of them ftood up, one after another, and made the refponfes, which the chaplain ex-plained to them.   After this he prayed, and the fervice con-cluded by finging the fifty-firft Pfalm.   The decent be-haviour and attention of the audience, evidently proved that the fervice, though of two hours and a half, was not tedious or difagreeable.

I cannot forbear clofing this account, with mentioning the ardent wifhes it infpired in me, that *our* prifons alfo, inftead of echoing with profanenefs and blafphemy, might hereafter refound with the offices of religious worfhip, and prove, like thefe, the happy means of awakening many to a fenfe of their *duty* to *God* and *man.**

At AMSTERDAM the prifon is in the Stadt-houfe. Debtors and felons quite feparate.   No court.   Vifitants
may

---

* On converfing with a fenfible magiftrate, his words were, " I have " known perfons who have come out of our houfes of correction thoroughly " reformed, and have thanked God for their confinement."

may converfe with debtors at the lattices of their rooms, from nine to twelve in the forenoon. The debtor may buy an anchor of wine to depofite with the keeper (who fells liquors): He is allowed to call for a bottle of it a day, paying the keeper two ftivers a bottle.

The rooms for criminals are down fifteen fteps; ten feet by nine: Each, for one prifoner only: A bedftead, &c. door-way twenty-two inches wide; door four inches thick: The condemned rooms have an iron door befides. In the latter a criminal is never left alone: Two prifoners from the rafp-houfe are always with him, to prevent his deftroying himfelf. They rejoice at the fervice; for if they difcharge it faithfully, their reward is an abridgement of their allotted term. The execution is generally performed within forty-eight hours after the fentence. From a book containing the names and crimes of all who have been executed at Amfterdam, from January 1693 to the end of 1766, the number amounts to 336. But only 25 were executed in the laft 20 years of that term. And I have been well informed, that in three years preceding my vifit in 1778, only one criminal was executed, and he was beheaded.

The children of the malefactors who are executed, are fent to the orphan-houfe, and there brought up in induftry, and not left deftitute vagabonds to become unhappy victims to the wickednefs and folly of their parents.

Prayers are read morning and evening, and before and after meals, by one of the beft-behaved convicts: And divine fervice, with a fermon, is performed by a clergyman on Sunday mornings.

The fpin-houfe is for women. This, and the workhoufe, are under the direction of fix regents and four governeffes,

verneffes, who appoint two fathers and two mothers to fu-
perintend and infpect the work, the diet, and the lodging
of the prifoners, and to chaftife the difobedient.

The work-room is a large room up ftairs, feparated by
a wooden baluftrade from the paffage (fix feet wide) into
which fpectators are admitted.   This room is divided by
baluftrades, into three, for diftinguifhing thofe who have
fuffered fome *public* or *corporal punifhment*, from the others
who have not been whipped, and expofed on a fcaffold.

In this houfe you fee a number of criminals (in 1776,
there were thirty-two ; in 1778, forty-fix) fome of whom
had been the moft abandoned, fitting in prefence of the
mother, quiet and orderly at their different forts of work;
fpinning, plain work &c.   Of the latter fort much is fent
in from the city.   They have the fame holidays as at the
Rafp-houfe.   Hours of work from fix to twelve, and from
one to eight.   I faw them go from work to dinner : the
keeper, or *father* as they call him, prefided.   Firft they
fung a pfalm: Then they went in order down to a neat dining-
room; where they feated themfelves at two tables; and
feveral difhes of boiled barley, agreeably fweetened, were
fet before them.   The father ftruck with a hammer: Then
in profound filence all ftood up; and one of them read with
propriety, a prayer about four or five minutes.   Then they
fat down cheerful; and each filled her bowl, from a large
difh, which contained enough for four of them.   Then one
brought on, a waiter, flices of bread and butter, and ferved
each prifoner.

The mother was feated at a defk (where fhe had a full
view of her family at work) with a Bible before her.

As I ftaid longer than a common vifitant, one of the prifoners

foners went up to the miftrefs with the timid modefty of a fuppliant, and afked leave to offer me the plate. The leave was granted. The miftrefs keeps what is given, till, it amounts to a fum fufficient to purchafe a little *tea* or *eoffce*, for all to partake.

This houfe is fupported by a fmall annual *tax* on thofe who fell tobacco, beer and other liquors, and *one fourth part* of what is received at *public exhibitions* and *diverfions*.

At the HAGUE I was honoured with the very polite affiftance of Sir Jofeph Yorke. A magiftrate accompanied me to the prifon, where all was quiet and in order. The fame gentleman prefented me with a *copy of inftructions* to the fheriff of the court; a *copy of rules* for officers of the attorney-general, and with a *M. S. copy* on feveral fheets, of forty-four rules for the management of the prifon.

At UTRECHT, in 1776, no prifoners in the Stadt-houfe; and in 1778, no debtors, and only one criminal, and his offence not capital. There has not been an execution for the city or province thefe fourteen years. The allowance for debtors, the firft week, is twenty-eight ftivers a day ; the fecond week, fixteen; and every day afterwards, eight ftivers. The ftate allows criminals, thirteen ftivers a day, which are paid to the gaoler. " For," as he told me, " confinement here is not meant as punifhment, but only " as fafe cuftody till trial. After which, fome who are " to be punifhed by a fhort imprifonment are fent to ano- " ther prifon, where they live on bread and water only." He faid a woman who had been his prifoner, was that day fentenced to be fo punifhed for a fortnight ; but he added, " She will have a fufficient quantity ; and if fhe be ill, her " food will be altered."

I

I leave this country with regret, as it affords a large field for information on the important fubject I have in view. I know not which to admire moft, the *neatnefs* and *cleanlinefs* appearing in the prifons, the *induftry* and *regular conduct* of the prifoners, or the *humanity* and *attention* of the magiftrates and regents.*

GERMANY.

THE Germans, well aware of the neceffity of *cleanlinefs* in prifons, have very judicioufly chofen to build them in fituations moft conducive to it; that is, *near rivers*: As at Hanover, Zell, Hamburgh, Berlin, Bremen, Cologn, Mentz, and many other places.

In the gaols that I firft faw, there were but few prifoners, except thofe called, improperly, *galley-flaves.* One caufe of this is a fpeedy trial after commitment.

The galley-flaves have every where a prifon to themfelves. They work on the *roads*, the *fortifications, chalk-hills*, and other public fervice; for four, feven, ten, fifteen, twenty years, according to their crimes; and are clothed, as well as fed, by the government. At Wefel, which belongs to the King of Pruffia, there were ninety-eight of thefe flaves: They have two pounds of bread a day, and the value of three halfpence Englifh every day they work.

I faw no under-ground dungeons in any of the *new* prifons in Germany, except at Liege; nor indeed in any
other

---

* I fhould accufe myfelf of ingratitude, did not I take this occafion again to exprefs my acknowledgements to Sir Jofeph Yorke, who, not only exerted himfelf with ardour to promote the fuccefs of my inquiries; but while I was confined at the Hague in confequence of an accident at my laft vifit, favoured me with inftances of kindnefs and friendfhip that I never can forget.

other *new* prifon abroad. At Lunenburg the dungeons are difufed; and inftead of them are built additional rooms up ftairs; one for each prifoner. And in moft of the gaols each criminal is alone in his room; which is more or lefs ftrong, lightfome, and airy, as the crime he is charged with is more or lefs atrocious.

One often fees the doors of fundry rooms marked Ethiopia, India, Italy, France, England, &c. In thofe rooms, parents, by the authority of the magiftrates, confine for a certain term diffolute children; and if they are inquired after, the anfwer is, they are gone to Italy, England, &c.

I do not remember any prifon in Germany, (nor elfewhere abroad) in which *felons* have not, either from the public allowance, or from charities, fomewhat more to live on than bread and water. In fome places a perfon goes on market-days with a bafket for prifoners; and I have feen him bring them a comfortable meal of frefh vegetables. But there are feparate prifons, in which confinement for a week or two on bread and water is all the punifhment for fome petty offences. Perhaps, when a condemned criminal is only to live a day or two, fuch diet may be more proper than the indulgence with which the Germans, and other foreigners treat prifoners after fentence of death, which is commonly executed within forty-eight hours. The malefactor has then his choice of food, and wine, in a commodious room, into which his friends are admitted; and a minifter attends him during almoft all his remaining hours.

I went into Germany in June 1778, by Ofnabrug and Hanover. The prifon at OSNABRUG I fhould entirely omit, did I not entertain a hope, that the account of it may poffibly engage the notice of an amiable *Prince* who is the

C 2

prefent

present *bishop*, and so be the means of alleviating the sufferings of the miserable prisoners. The prison and the house of correction is one large building, situated in an airy part of the suburbs, near a brook. A Latin inscription over the gate implies, that it was erected " at the public expence, in 1756, for the purposes of public justice and utility, by confining and punishing the wicked."—There are seventeen chambers for criminals, which have no light but by a small aperture over each door. I was happy to find *here* no more than one prisoner. He had been confined three years, and had survived the cruelty of the torture. In *another part* of the house I found many miserable and sickly objects, men, women, and children, almost all without shoes and stockings. They were spinning in different rooms, which were dirty beyond description. These rooms open into an offensive passage, which a gentleman in office in the city, to whom I was recommended, durst not enter. I inquired of the keeper concerning several particulars in the diet, &c. but the misery expressed in the *countenances* of the prisoners, made me totally disregard the information given me by words.

The prison at HANOVER was built about thirty years ago. It is situated on the river Leyna. There are eleven strong rooms about ten feet square, and ten and a half high; with a bed of solid stone in each, eleven inches from the ground, and nine inches higher at the head. Over these are larger apartments for debtors, &c. The rooms are warmed by stoves in winter. Criminals have a small chain: They are allowed straw to lie on, and two coverlets. When I visited the prison in 1776, there were seven criminals and one debtor; and in 1778, two debtors and three criminals. The keeper sells no liquors, but has a salary. In the council-chamber are all the various edicts in frames. There is a torture-chamber; but I with pleasure

learned

learned that the two cruel engines had not been ufed for four years.

At HAMBURGH, the *felons* in the *Buttelcy* were all in irons. The common method of execution is decollation. The executioner, who is gaoler, fhewed me the fword which, he faid, he had made ufe of eight times.

Among the various engines of torture, or the queftion, which I have feen in France, Italy, Germany, and other places, one of the moft excruciating is kept and ufed in a deep cellar of this prifon. It ought to be buried ten thoufand fathom deeper. It is faid the inventor was the firft who fuffered by it: The laft was a woman, a few years ago.

Here, as at fome other towns, is a prifon for flight offences. The punifhment, to be confined from a week to a month, and live on bread and water only. To prevent the prifoners having any thing elfe, what money they bring with them is taken, and fealed up; but it is returned to them when difcharged.

At BREMEN, the prifon for debtors has four rooms; but the magiftrate who accompanied me, Dr Hornwinckel, affured me not one of them had been occupied for above thirty years, till very lately, when one was fitted up for a debtor, who was confined in it a few weeks.

I fat an afternoon with Dr Duntze, of Bremen, who told me he was in London in 1753 and 54, with an inquifitive friend, a German. They went into Newgate to obferve the effects of the *ventilator*, and were ftruck with an offenfive fmell in one of the rooms. Next day they were both indifpofed. The Doctor's complaint turned out a kind of
jaundice.

jaundice. After a few days confinement he vifited his friend, and found him exceflively low; and in a fhort time he died with every fymptom of the *gaol fever.*

At BERLIN, in the city prifon, called *Calandfhof*, were eighteen men and thirteen women in fifteen rooms, in each of which was a ftove. The men and women have the ufe of the court at different hours. The allowance to each is one grofche and twelve pfennigs, about two-pence three farthings, a day. There is a chapel. There is no torture-room in any of the prifons in the Pruflian dominions, for the prefent king has fet the example in Germany of abolifh-ing the cruel practice.

At DRESDEN, the apartments for the flaves being under the fortifications, muft be unhealthy. I faw four fick, and yet they had their irons on. Among thofe that were at work, one had an iron collar, by way of punifhment, for making an efcape, befides the broad iron about his leg. Another was fitting, and endeavouring fomewhat to alter the place of his iron. He told me, that the weight was marked on it *twenty-one pounds*, and that he could not have it changed to the other leg without paying a fmith.

At VIENNA I vifited all the prifons, and moft of the hofpitals. The prifons are old buildings, and afford no inftruction.

The front of the great prifon, *La Maifon du Bourreau*, is remarkable for a very ftriking reprefentation of the cru-cifixion of our Saviour and the two thieves on mount Cal-vary. In this prifon are many horrid dungeons.[*]

At

---

[*] Here, as ufual, I inquired whether they had any putrid fever, and was anfwered in the nagative. But in one of the dark dungeons down twenty-four

At TRIESTE, the prison consists of eight or ten very close offensive rooms, each having only one small window. The pale countenances of the nineteen prisoners bespoke their own misery, and the negligence of the magistrates and keepers: But in the Castle were eighty-five slaves (*Condannati*). They appeared healthy, clean, and strong, and laboured cheerfully, because when they were employed, each of them received, as extraordinary pay, three farthings a day. They were treated with humanity, though under strict discipline; were well supplied with food and cloths; had two shirts, two pair of stockings, &c. and they lay in good beds.*

I T A L Y.

I entered Italy with raised expectations of considerable information, from a careful attention to the prisons and hospitals, in a country abounding with charitable institutions, and public edifices.

At

four steps, I thought I had found a person with the gaol fever. He was loaded with heavy irons, and chained to the wall: Anguish and misery appeared with clotted tears on his face. He was not capable of speaking to me; but on examining his breast and feet for *petechiæ* or spots, and finding he had a strong intermitting pulse, I was convinced that he was not ill of that disorder. A prisoner in an opposite cell told me, that the poor creature had desired him to call out for assistance, and he had done it, but was not heard. This is one of the *bad effects* of dungeons.

* May not one great cause of the unhealthiness of our prisoners be, the want of proper bedding, which obliges them to lie in their cloths? How different did these prisoners appear at the *castle* from many that I have seen in Prussia, and at Vienna! I was struck with the same good appearance of the *women* prisoners at several of the spin houses in Holland. This reminds me of what I heard an old *general* say, "That he always found his men subject to illness " and diseases when they lay in camps, *not* from *dampness*, but from *lying* " *in their cloths* and the *want* of *proper bedding*; for at the same time all " his officers had been quite healthy and well." Whatever be the *cause* of " this difference, whether a *more free perspiration* in bed, *taking off band-* " *ages*, or *ventilation of the cloths*, I am fully convinced of the *fact*.

At Venice, the great prifon is near the *Doge's* palace, and it is one of the ftrongeft I ever faw. There were between three and four hundred prifoners, many of them confined in loathfome and *dark* cells for life ; executions here being very rare. There was no fever, or prevailing diforder in this clofe prifon. None of the prifoners had irons. On weighing the bread allowance, I found it fourteen ounces. I afked fome who had been confined many years in dark cells, whether they fhould prefer the galleys? They all anfwered in the affirmative: So great a blefling is light and air! The chapel is only for the *condemned*, who continue there a night and a day before execution.

One of the *galleys* was moored two boats' length from the fhore, in which were only twenty-feven flaves, who were kept here in order to be fent on board the other galleys. This was clean. Here, and in the *other galleys*, which were dirty and crowded the flaves were in chains of about twenty-feven pounds weight.*

In Florence are two prifons. In the great prifon, *Palazzo degl' Otto*, were only twenty prifoners. Six of them were in the *fecret* chambers, which are twenty-one ftrong rooms. None of the prifoners were in irons. They had matreffes to lie on. Their bread was good. In the torture-chamber, there was a machine for decollation, which prevents that repetition of the ftroke which too often happens when the axe is ufed.†

In

* I faw a flave dead on the fhore, who I fuppofe deftroyed himfelf in defpair; for he could not hope to efcape by fwimming, becaufe of his heavy irons.

† I cannot leave Florence without exprefling my great obligation to the Grand Duke for his permiffion to infpect the prifons; and making my acknowledgements to Sir Horace Mann our ambaffador, for his very kind attention and affiftance.

In the prifon at LEGHORN were three *debtors*, and eight of thofe called *prifoners at large*, and in the *fecrete* three criminals.   I mention this prifon becaufe of the infirma- ry, which, as appears by an infcription over the door, was built at the expence of the prefent governor, Philip Bor- bonio, in 1761.

ROME.—In the prifon at the *Capital* are two rooms for poor *debtors*, and for criminals whofe offences are not fo great as to caufe them to be confined in the *fecrete*.   The prifoners in one of thefe rooms, have the privilege of afk- ing alms of the paffengers. There were five *debtors* in rooms which they paid for, and two *criminals* in the *fecrete*. This prifon is not offenfive.   There is a conftant current of wa- ter through one of the large rooms.

The ftate prifoners are confined in the caftle of *San. Angelo.* The rooms appropriated to that purpofe were all empty, except one, in which was a *bifhop*, who had been confined upwards of twenty years, and was diftracted. Here were alfo eighteen *condannati*, who work in the for- trefs, and had each a light chain. They feemed healthy and well.

On the death of the *Pope*, the prifoners are brought hi- ther from the great prifon, for upon fuch occafions the prifons are thoroughly cleaned.

I can give but little information refpecting the prifon of the inquifition. It is fituated near the great church of St Peter's. On one fide of the court round which it is built, is the inquifitor-general's palace. Over the gate is an in- fcription importing " that it was erected by Pope Pius V.
D   in

in the year 1569." The windows of the prifon have wooden blinds, and at a fmall diftance is a high wall.*

In this city, and many others in Italy, is a *Confraternita della mifericordia*, called *S. Giovanni di Fiorentini.* It confifts of about feventy, chiefly nobles, of the beft families. After a prifoner is condemned, one or two of them come to him the *midnight* before his execution, inform him of the fentence, and continue with him till his death They, with the confeffor, exhort and comfort him, and give him his choice of the moft delicious food. All the *fraternity* attend the execution, dreffed in white. When the prifoner is dead, they leave him hanging till the evening; then one of the *fraternity*, generally a *prince*, cuts him down, and orders him to be conveyed to the burying place which they have appropriated to malefactors. I was there the twenty-ninth of Auguft, the only day in the year when this burying-place is opened to the public.—Adjoining an elegant church is a chapel, which makes, one fide of a court, and on each of the other three fides, is a portico fupported by Doric pillars. In the middle of the pavement of the front portico the *women*, and in one of the fide portico's the *men* are buried. The latter are interred in the fame drefs in which they were hanged; for in Italy, coffins are not in general ufe.

The pope's galleys are CIVITA-VECCHIA. The flaves condemned to them are confined for different terms, according to the nature of their crimes; but the fhorteft time is three years for vagabonds, who are generally employed on board the pontons in clearing the harbour. For theft, the

---

* The chambers of this *filent* and *melancholy* abode were quite inacceffible to me; and yet I fpent near two hours about the court and priefts' apartments, till my continuance here began to raife fufpicion.

the term is never under feven years. Perfons convicted of forgery are always confined for life; and if found guilty of forging bank-notes, or any inftruments by which large fums have been loft, they are punifhed with an *iron glove.* Prifoners *for life* are chained two and two together; thofe for *limited terms* have all a fingle chain, and, at their firft arrival, of the fame weight; but when they have no more than one or two years to ferve, they have only a ring round their leg, which is leffened as the end of their term approaches. For efcapes, they are obliged to finifh their *firft* condemnation, and then receive a frefh one for the fame time as the former; but if the firft was for life, the fame is renewed, and they receive from a hundred to two hundred lafhes a day, for three days after their arrival. *None are fent to the galleys under the age of twenty :* Criminals of a younger age are kept at the hofpital of S. *Michele* in Rome till they are of age; and are there employed in fpinning, and fed on bread and water.

The principal prifon in the great and populous city NA-PLES is *La Vicaria,* under the courts of juftice. It contained when I was there, according to the gaoler's account, nine hundred and eighty prifoners. In about eight large rooms, communicating with one another, there were five hundred and forty fickly objects, who had accefs to a court furrounded by buildings fo high as to prevent the circulation of air. In feven clofe offenfive rooms were thirty-one prifoners, almoft without cloths, on account of the great heat; and in fix dirty rooms, communicating with one another, were fifty *women.* Of all the prifoners, one *man* only was in irons, in a dungeon, near a fmall chapel, which is allotted to the condemned before execution.

The great and crowded hofpitals of S. *Apoftoli* and
L'Annun-

L'Annunziazione, have wards appropriated to the cure of wounded perfons.*

The hofpital of the *Benfratelli*, or *S. Gio di Dio*, is clean and elegant. It confifts chiefly of one lofty ward ; at one end of which is an altar and a room for poor priefts ; and at the other end, a table, on which are placed the patients' victuals. Near this table was infcribed a reference to the appofite words of Scripture, *Matthew* xxv. 35, 36. *For I was an hungred, and ye gave me meat, &c.*

In many of the Italian hofpitals, and *in all* that I have feen belonging to this order of friars, there are *no rooms* over the fick wards, fo that they are as *lofty* as our churches or chapels.

At GENOA, befides a prifon for *debtors*, and a prifon for *female criminals*, there is a great prifon for *male criminals*, confifting of thirty-five rooms. I faw none of the prifoners in irons. Their daily allowance was thirteen ounces of good wheaten bread for each, befides foup. To this prifon belongs an hofpital and a chapel, with a large room to which the condemned are brought four days before their exe-

---

* The frequency of affaults and affaffinations in Italy is generally known. Many of the common people feem to be infenfible of the atrocioufnefs of the crime of murder. I have heard criminals in prifon exprefs, with feeming fatisfaction of mind, " that tho' they ftabbed, they did not rob." If we confider that wards and even hofpitals appropriated to the wounded are filled with patients, that the prifons are crowded, and that many are continually taking refuge on the fteps of churches, and examine our accounts in *Janffen's Lifts* and the *Judges' Returns*, we may reckon that there are more murders committed in a year in the city of Naples or Rome, than in Great Britain and Ireland. Does not this prove that the Englifh are not naturally cruel ? And might not arguments be derived from hence, for the revifal and repeal of fome of our fanguinary laws ? The Marquis Beccaria juftly remarks, in his *Effay on Crimes and Punifhments*, chap. 28. " That the punifhment of " death is pernicious to fociety, from the example of barbarity it affords."

execution.—The *inſtructions* formed for this priſon by the ſupreme ſyndics, are hung up in it, and contain good regulations, as will appear from the following account of a few of them,

" The keeper ſhall have under him ſix aſſiſtants :—and the ſaid keeper is to be reſponſible, and liable to puniſhment, if any of the aſſiſtants ſhall be guilty of the leaſt fraud or neglect in their employment.—The advocate fiſcal is once a week, at any time he ſhall think proper, *but when he is leaſt expected*, to viſit the cells of the priſon, and to enquire diligently how the priſoners are treated by the keeper and aſſiſtants, in order to give information to the moſt *ſerene ſenate*, &c.—When any priſoner is condemned to death, he is immediately to be put into chains.—The keeper is always to keep the chapel ſhut, except at the time of celebrating maſs, confeſſion, or *adminiſtering conſolation* to the unhappy.—He is alſo to take care that the priſoners do not play at any *games*, particularly *cards*. The laſt order is, that this table of regulations be fixed up in the criminal court of juſtice, in the chancery, and in the apartments of the criminals."

At CHAMBERRY I found that the ſalutary practice of waſhing the priſon was adopted. Beſides the ſtated allowance of good bread, the priſoners are often ſupplied with bread and ſoup, and in winter with cloths and coverlets, by a charitable ſociety of ladies. In one of the rooms I ſaw chains, but was told they had not been uſed ſince the walls had been built higher. A diſmal torture-chamber, into which day-light never enters, makes a part of this priſon.

Before the Cantons, I will mention, what is not indeed
any

any part of Switzerland, the little Republic of

G E N E V A.

In the prifon, which was formerly the bifhop's palace,
at my firft vifit, there were only five *criminals*; none of
them in irons.   Their allowance about fix-pence a day;
for which they have a pound of good bread, fome foup,
and half a pint of wine.   They looked healthy.   Here, as
in the Swifs Cantons, men and women are kept feparate.
For fome years paft, no capital punifhment.   If a criminal
flies from juftice, they call him in form three days; and
after trial, execute him in effigy.

There feldom are any debtors.   A creditor muft allow
his debtor in prifon as much as felons have from the public: Upon failure, the gaoler gives notice, and then dif-
charges the prifoner.   Befides, there are *fumptuary* laws
in this ftate.   And though the government is in general
mild, there is a fevere law againft bankrupts, and infol-
vents, which renders incapable of all honours, and deprives
of freedom, not only the debtor himfelf, but his children
after him; except fuch of them as pay their quota of the
debts.

At my laft vifit, there were two debtors, and five other
prifoners; to whom great attention was paid, as they were
then laying new floors in the lower rooms, left they fhould
be damp and injurious to their health.*

In

* I hoped to have found here no torture-chambers, but I had only the pleafure to hear that none had fuffered in them thefe twenty-five years.   They
are thus reftrained by the thirty-fecond article in the *Reglement de l'illuftre
Mediation pour la Pacification des troubles de la Republique de Geneve,* publifhed in 1738.   " *Les accufes et criminels ne pourront etre, appliques a la Quef-*
" *tion ou Torture, que prealablement ils n'ayent ete par jugement definitif,*
" *condamnes a mort.*"

In entering Switzerland from Geneva, a traveller will be surprised to meet frequently with a gibbet on the road, if he be not informed that almost every *seigneurie* or bailliwick has a prison, and possesses the power of trying criminals, and capitally convicting them. I visited one of these prisons. It belonged to Mr Baron de Prangins, and consisted of four rooms at the top of his castle. It was empty.

In those of the Cantons to which I went, *felons* have each a room to themselves, " that they may not," said the keepers, " *tutor one another.*" None were in irons; they are kept in rooms more or less strong and lightsome, according to the crimes they are charged with. In some Cantons there were no prisoners of this sort. The principal reason of it is, the great care that is taken to give children, even the poorest, a moral and religious education. Another thing which contributes to the same intention, is the laudable police of speedy justice. A criminal has notice of his death, not the manner of it, but a short time before he is to suffer; and he is then indulged with his choice of food, wine, &c. Women are not hanged, but beheaded. Every new executioner has a new sword; and in the arsenal at Bern I saw several old ones hung up in order. In the houses of correction, many of the prisoners were women, whom I saw at work.

At LAUSANNE I visited the prison, in which there were, at that time, no prisoners. There were dungeons; but on entering each of them, the keeper observed, that we were not yet upon the ground, but there were cellars underneath. On conversing with Dr Tissot, he expressed his surprise at our gaol distemper; said, " I should not find it in Switzerland:" And added, that " he had not heard of its being any where but in England." When I mentioned the late act for preserving the health of our prisoners, he ap-

approved of it highly, especially the clause which required *white-washing the rooms, and keeping them clean.*—I did
not (as the doctor said) find the gaol fever in Switzerland :
Nor did I find it any where else abroad.*

At BERN, the principal Canton, there were no prisoners
but in the two houses of correction.   One of these prisons
is for citizens, in which the men and women were spinning, for they never work abroad.

In *La Prison Ordinaire*, some rooms are planked all
round.   Eight of them are very close and strong.   Doors
of oak two inches and a half thick, plated with iron ; three
hinges, a lock and two padlocks.   In a closet, were the
cloths of a person that was murdered, kept to confront the
guilty when apprehended : And some stolen goods, to be
owned.   A criminal who can pay is allowed to expend 7
batz 2 *creutzers*, about a shilling, daily, for two meals of
soup and good bread.   To one that is poor, the government allows half that sum.   To all who are condemned,
they allow a shilling a day for eight days before they suffer.   These allowances are specified on a paper hung up in
the gaol.   There also hangs up a serious exhortation concerning the awful nature of an *oath;* and the forms of sun-
dry oaths to be taken.   I procured copies of the whole,
but

* Sir John Pringle, President of the Royal Society, in his *Discourse* at the
Anniversary Meeting, 30th November, 1776, informs us at page 16, that
" The late Dr Mounsey, F. R. S. who had lived long in Russia, and had been
" *Archiater* under two successive sovereigns—happening to be at Moscow
" when he perused the *Observations on the Gaol Fever*—was induced to com-
" pare what he read in that Treatise with what he should see in the several
" prisons of that large city : But to his surprise, after visiting them all, and
" finding them full of malefactors (for the late Empress then suffered none
" —to be put to death) he could discover no fever among them, nor learn
" that any acute distemper peculiar to gaols had ever been known there.—
" Upon his return to St Petersburg, he made the same inquiry there, and with
" the same result."

but will tranſcribe only one oath, as follows :—" *Ma de-*
" *poſition, dont lecture m'a ete faite, a preſent, je la confirme*
" *devant la face du Dieu tout puiſſant, tout ſechant et vray,*
" *pour contenir la verite, ainſi que je deſire que Dieu me ſoit*
" *en aide ſur la fin de mes jours. Sans dol ni fraude..*"—
" My depoſition, which has now been read to me, I con-
" firm before the face of God omnipotent, omniſcient and
" true, to contain the truth, as I deſire that God may be
" my help at the end of my days. Without deceit or
" fraud." Perjury, I was told, is very uncommon among
them.

In this city I had ſome diſcourſe with the celebrated
Dr Haller. He aſcribed the ſickneſs in Engliſh gaols to
their being over-crowded.

At BASIL, the gaol for felons is one of the towers. No
priſoners; but many rooms ready with clean ſtraw and
blankets. Each priſoner (they ſaid) has a room to himſelf, in which he is conſtantly ſhut up, except when conducted to the council-chamber for examination. One of
the ſtrongeſt cells is in a room by the great clock, and is
about ſix feet high : The trap door is in the flat roof ; the
priſoner goes down by a ladder, which is then taken up ;
his victuals are put in a wicket on one ſide. When I was
in the room, and took notice of the uncommon ſtrength
of it, the gaoler told me a priſoner had lately made his
eſcape from it. I could not deviſe what method he took,
but heard it was this. He had a ſpoon for ſoup, which he
ſharpened to cut out a piece from the timber of his room:
then by practice he acquired the knack of ſtriking his door,
juſt when the great clock ſtruck (to drown the noiſe): and
in fifteen days he forced all the bolts, &c. But attempting
to let himſelf down from the vaſt height by a rope which he
found, the rope failed him ; and by falling he broke ſo

E   many

many of his bones, that the furgeons pronounced his recovery impoffible. But his bones were fet; and with proper care he did recover, and was pardoned.

From Switzerland I returned into Germany, to vifit fome prifons which I had not feen, particularly thofe in the *free* or *imperial Cities*.

G E R M A N Y.

At Augsburg, the prifon is on the fide of a hill, at the back of the town-houfe. It confifts of many *cachots* or fmall rooms, on three different floors. There is one for examination, and two for the engines of torture.* The condemned are brought three days before their execution into two light rooms, which open into a Roman catholic chapel: where, however, if a prifoner be a Proteftant, a Lutheran minifter is permitted to attend him.

The *houfe of corrcction* confifts of buildings on *two* fides of a fpacious court; *one* fide for thofe of the Roman catholic religion, and the *other* for Proteftants, with a chapel for each. The rooms were all clean, and are white-wafhed every year. Oppofite to the front windows in moft of the rooms, were high windows, of a femicircular form, which were defigned for promoting a circulation of air.

At Munich or *Munchen*, there are two prifons for criminals. That in the town-houfe, had in it fix men and two women prifoners. In a dark damp dungeon down feventeen fteps, were the inftruments of torture.

The

---

* There are alfo two dark dungeons for fuch as have been convicted of witchcraft: But they are in a very ruihous condition, and feem to have been a long time without inhabitants.

The other, called *La Prifon de la Cour*, confifted of about fifteen cells, twelve feet by feven, and a black torture-room. *

In the *houfe of correction* were about forty men and thirty women; fome *weaving* wide cloth, but moft of them *fpinning*. The keeper ordered his fervant to attend me with charcoal and frankincenfe; a certain fign of negligence and inattention, which the countenances of the prifoners confirmed.

I was agreeably relieved from the pain excited by thefe fcenes, with the view of the two hofpitals of *Les Freres* and *Les Sœurs de Charite*. In the former were about forty beds; in the latter twenty: The wards were about twenty-fix feet wide. All was neat and clean, ftill and quiet; and the great attention paid to the patients was every where apparent. I faw the operation of bleeding performed by the *Nuns* with great dexterity and tendernefs. Over the foot of each bed a text of Scripture was infcribed, as in fome Italian hofpitals.

E 2   At

* In this room there is a table covered with black cloth and fringe. Six chairs for the magiftrates and fecretaries, covered alfo with black cloth, are elevated two fteps above the floor, and painted black. Various engines of torture, fome of which are ftained with blood, hang round the room. When the criminals fuffer, the candles are lighted; for the windows are fhut clofe, to prevent their cries being heard abroad. Two crucifixes are prefented to the view of the unhappy objects. But it is too fhocking to relate their different modes of cruelty. Even women are not fpared.—This room feems much like the torture-room in Spain, defcribed in Limborch's *Hiftory of the Inquifition*, tranflated by Chandler, vol. II. p. 221, 4to. edit. " It was a large " under-ground room, arched, and the walls covered with black hangings. " The candlefticks were faftened to the wall, and the whole room enlight- " ened with candles placed in them.—The inquifitor and notary fat at a table, " fo that the place feemed as the very manfion of death, every thing appear- " ing fo terrible and awful."

At MANHEIM, Monfieur Babo, counfellor to the regen-cy, very politely gave orders to fhew me every room of *La Maifon de Force.* Prifoners committed to this houfe are commonly received in form with what is called the *bien venu* (welcome). A machine is brought out, in which are faftened their neck, hands, and feet. Then they are ftripped; and have, according as the magiftrate orders—the *grand venu* of twenty or thirty ftripes—the *demi venu* of eighteen to twenty—or the *petit venu* of twelve to fif-teen; after this they kifs the threfhold and go in. Some are treated with the fame compliment at difcharge. The like ceremony is obferved at many other towns in Ger-many.

The *rules* and *orders* are good. I have a copy of them. The two laft are to this effect. 11th. As it is of the utmoft importance in fuch houfes as this, to obferve all poffible cleanlinefs; it is required of all perfons to watch moft ftrictly againft all appearance of the contrary. Whoever fees the leaft offence of that kind, fhall give immediate no-tice of it to the *infpector*, upon pain of clofe confinement on bread and water, and the moft rigorous chaftifement. 12th. That no one may be able to plead ignorant of the rules, one copy of them fhall be *given* to every prifoner, and another *hung up* in his room; and they fhall be *read publicly* every Sunday morning after divine fervice. It is ordered that the difobedient be punifhed; and that encou-ragement be given to the dutiful and diligent.

A capuchin fays mafs in the chapel every morning. A galley for men; another for women, with a blind before it; another for *orphans*, of whom there are fixty-four in a fort of hofpital at one end of the prifon. Proteftants and Jews are ordered to their private devotions; the latter are ex-cufed from working on their *fabbath.*

Every

Every prifon at MENTZ has in each room a German ftove; which, in winter, is heated two or three times a day. Prifoners have clean linen once a week. On my obferving to the Brigadier of the Police who went with me, how healthy his prifon looked, he told me that " Some " years ago, they were unhealthy; and the regency re- " moved them from the dungeons; upon which they re- " covered; and had been remarkably healthy ever fince." The dungeons are now totally difufed.

The two prifons (diftinguifhed by the names of the *old* and the *new*) *La Porte de St Leonard* in LIEGE, are on the ramparts.—In two rooms of the *old* prifon I faw fix cages made very ftrong with iron hoops, four of which were empty. Thefe were difmal places of confinement; but I foon found worfe. In defcending deep below ground from the gaoler's apartments, I heard the moans of the miferable wretches in the dark dungeons. The fides and roof were all ftone. In wet weather, water from the *foffes* gets into them, and has greatly damaged the floors. Each of them had two fmall apertures, one for admitting air, and the other, with a fhutter over it ftrongly bolted, for putting in food to the prifoners. One dungeon larger than the reft was appropriated to the fick. In looking into this, with a candle, I difcovered a ftove, and felt fome furprife at this little efcape of humanity from the men who conftructed thefe cells.

The dungeons in the *new* prifon are abodes of mifery ftill more fhocking; and confinement in them fo over-powers human nature, as fometimes irrecoverably to take away the fenfes. I heard the cries of the diftracted as I went down to them. One woman, however, I faw, who (as I was told) had fuftained this horrid confinement forty-feven years without becoming diftracted.

The

The cries of the sufferers in the torture-chamber may be heard by passengers without, and guards are placed to prevent them from stopping and listening. A physician and surgeon always attend when the torture is applied; and on a signal given by a bell, the gaoler brings in wine, vinegar and water to prevent the sufferers from expiring.—— " *The tender mercies of the wicked are cruel.*" Thus in the Spanish inquisition, the physician and surgeon attend to determine the utmost extremity of suffering without expiring under the torture.

I will only add, that in this prison there are rooms appropriated to prisoners *en pension*; that is, to such as are confined by the magistrates, at the desire of their parents, guardians or relations. A shocking practice! which prevails also in some of the neighbouring countries.

A U S T R I A N   F L A N D E R S.

In the Austrian Netherlands I found the prisons in general clean; and no sickness prevailing in any one of them: And yet few of the prisons have a court: In most of them every prisoner is confined to his room.

In the prison at ANTWERP there are two rooms for citizens; and up stairs there is a cage, about six feet and a half square, into which criminals are put before the torture. A criminal, while he suffers the torture, is clothed in a long shirt, has his eyes bound, and a physician and surgeon attend him: And when a confession is forced from him, and wine has been given him, he is required to sign his confession; and about forty-eight hours afterwards he is executed.

In a small dungeon is a stone seat like some I have seen in

in old prifon towers, in which it is faid that formerly prifoners were *fuffocated by brimftone*, when their families wifhed
to avoid the difgrace of a public execution. No perfon here
remembers an inftance of this kind; but about thirty years
ago there was a *private* execution in the prifon. In this
prifon there were only two prifoners.

The *houfe of correction* for the *city of* GHENT is not fo
commodioufly built, nor kept fo clean as fome other Fle-
mifh prifons: But there are very good *rules* of economy,
of which I have a copy. Every prifoner is examined at his
firft coming; and if he be not healthy, he is not put among
thofe that are fo. That the keeper may not be tempted to
opprefs his prifoners, he is *exempted* from all taxes. The
prifoners have a fet tafk of different forts of work: The pro-
fits of extra-work their own. The magiftrates meet in the
prifon once a week to infpect it; and to appoint the fort
and quantity of provifion for every day of the week enfu-
ing. They order the phyfician to fee that the fick have
broth, and other nourifhment proper for them. The keeper provides it, and is paid by the magiftrates. I happened
to go into the prifon while they were there, and faw them
employed as above.

I fhall beg leave here, on account of the humanity of its
inftitution, to digrefs from my fubject by taking notice of
a nunnery in this place. The *hofpitable manfion* is not in-
habited folely by nuns; it is deftined to the reception of
men who are infane, and fick aged women. The infane
have, when requifite, affiftance from their own fex; and
the tendernefs with which both thefe and the poor women
are treated by the fifters, gave me no little pleafure.

FRENCH

FRENCH FLANDERS *and* FRANCE.

The French provinces in Flanders and the Netherlands, are chiefly governed by the fame *arret de parlement* as the provinces in France.

I vifited the prifons at LISLE, but found nothing worthy of imitation. *La Prifon Royale* is under no proper regulation; and the unhealthy countenances of the prifoners at the citadel, intimate the pernicious effects of lying in damp rooms, under the fortifications.

The two hofpitals *La Comteffe* and *St Sauveur* are lofty buildings, defigned only for the admiffion of *men;* for in this city there are no hofpitals for fick *women.* The patients are diftinguifhed into three forts, *viz.* wounded—very fick—and recovering; they have different wards affigned them accordingly, every patient has a bed to himfelf. Here cleanlinefs is the agreeable effect of the great attention given to the patients by the *nuns.*

In the prifon at ARRAS I obferved one circumftance which was different from what I had feen in France. Of one hundred and thirty-nine prifoners, I faw two in the court who had irons. But upon afking one of them the reafon of it, he told me " it was for attempting an efcape."

At AMIENS are two prifons; one for *Les Burgeois et Le Libertinage;* the other, *La Conciergerie.*—In the townhoufe, I faw great numbers attending the trial of a woman for confining her fon. He was then about thirty-two years of age, and had been confined fixteen years, with a feverity which had almoft deprived him of his intellects. The profecution was carried on by his father's relations, who

who had been long vigoroufly urgent for the releafe of him.

In or near PARIS are the *Conciergerie, Grand* and *Petit Chatelet, Fort L'Eveque, L'Abbaye*, and the *Bicetre*.

My firft queftion in each prifon commonly was, Whether the goaler or keeper refided in the houfe? and the anfwer was always in the affirmitive.

Moft prifons in the city have three or four doors, from four feet to four and a half high, feparated from each other by a little area or court. Within the inner door is in fome prifons, a *turnftile*. The number and lownefs of the doors (at each of which you muft ftoop) and the turnftiles, effectually prevent the prifoners rufhing out.

In moft of the prifons there are five or fix *turnkeys; viz.* two or three at the doors: One walking in the court, to prevent conferring and plotting (a circumftance to which French goalers are very attentive): One at the womens' ward: And every day one of them is abroad, or otherwife at leifure. This liberty they have in rotation. They are ftrictly prohibited, under fevere penalties, from receiving any thing of the prifoners, directly or indirectly, on any pretence whatever. The gaoler is obliged to board them; and pay to each of them at leaft one hundred *livres* a year.

I was furprifed at feeing that none of the prifoners were in *irons*. No gaoler (I was informed) may put them on a prifoner, without an exprefs order from the judge. And yet in fome of the prifons, there were more criminals than in any of our London gaols. When I was firft there, the number had been recently increafed by an infurrection on account of the fcarcity of corn. My reader will perhaps

F

prefently

prefently fee reafon to conclude, that the manner in which prifons are conducted makes the confinement more tolerable, and chains lefs needful. Indeed it was evident, from the very appearance of the prifoners in moft of the gaols, that *humane* attention was paid to them.

Moft of the courts are paved ; and they are wafhed three or four times a day. One would hardly believe how this frefhens the air in the upper rooms, I felt this very fenfibly once, and again when I was in the chambers : And an Englifhman, who had the misfortune to be a prifoner, made the fame remark. I feldom or never found in any French prifon that offenfive fmell which I had often perceived in Englifh gaols. I fometimes thought thefe courts were the cleaneft places in Paris. One circumftance that contributes to it, befides the number of turnkeys, is, that moft of them are near the river.

To prevent the frequent confequences of defperation, no one condemned to death by the inferior court, is without hopes of life, till the parliament, to which he commonly appeals, confirms or reverfes the fentence: And they never make known their decifion, till the morning of the day on which a prifoner is to fuffer, then they publifh a confirmation of the former fentence ; and it is fold in the ftreets. Executions are often in the afternoon : The laft that I faw was by torch light.

Taking *garnifh*, or footing, is ftrictly prohibited, if prifoners demand of a new comer any thing of that fort, on whatever pretence ; if, in order to obtain it, they diftrefs him by hiding his cloths, &c. they are fhut up for a fortnight in a dark dungeon, and fuffer other punifhment. They are obnoxious to the fame chaftifement for hiding one another's cloths, or been otherwife injurious.

The

The daily allowance to criminals is a Pound and a half of good bread, and fome foup. The foup is not made, nor is any other provifion drefled in the prifons. They have clean linen once a week, from a *fociety*, which was inftituted about the year 1753. The occafion of it was the prevalence of a contagious difeafe, which in France they call *le fcorbut*, the fcurvy. This diftemper was found to proceed from the prifons; and to fpread in the *Hotel Dieu*, whither prifoners that had it were removed. The caufe of it was generally thought to be *want of cleanlinefs in prifons*; where feveral of thofe confined had worn their linen for many months, and infected the moft healthy new-comers that were put in the room with them. Eight hundred were ill of it at once in the hofpital of St Louis, to which all that were fick of it in the *Hotel Dieu* had been carried. By the Abbé Breton's exerting himfelf on this occafion, a fund was raifed to fupport prifoners in the *Grand Chatelet* with clean linen every week. This put an effectual ftop to the malady in that prifon. Numbers afterwards joined the fociety: the King and Queen honoured it with their contributions: And the charity extended to three other prifons; fo that at laft feven hundred prifoners were provided for in the fame manner, and a ftock of linen requifite for that purpofe, *viz.* five thoufand fhirts, was completed. The elder prifoners have charge of the linen that is in the prifon; they receive it (every Saturday) and return it, and are gratified by the fociety; which continues to the prefent time. Befides this, there is fcarce a prifon in the city that has not a patronefs; a lady of character, who voluntarily takes care that thofe in the infirmaries be properly attended; gives them drugs; fupplies them with fuel, and linen; does many kind offices to the prifoners in general; and by foliciting the charity of others, procures not only the relief and comforts mentioned already, but foup twice a week, and meat once a fortnight.

There

There is alfo annually at each prifon fome what like our charity fermons; public fervice in the chapel, and a collection. On thefe occafions the patronefs attends; as I faw at Chriftmas, 1778, and foon after found the prifoners fupplied with cloths.

All the regulations are read in the chapel to prifoners, the firft Sunday of every month, by the chaplain; and they hang up in the prifon for common infpection. If any prifoner tears, or otherwife damages them, he fuffers corporal punifhment; If a regifter or gaoler does fo, he is fined twenty *livres*. If a turnkey, he is difcharged.

The turnkeys vifit the dungeons four times a day; in the morning when the prifons were opened, at noon, at fix in the evening, and at ten at night. I was forry to find the humanity which is fo confpicuous in the forementioned, and other excellent rules, fo deficient as to continue the ufe of thofe fubterraneous abodes; which are totally dark, and beyond imagination horrid and dreadful. Poor creatures are confined in them night and day for weeks, for months together. If the turnkeys find any prifoners fick, they muft acquaint the phyfician and furgeon, who vifit them; and if needful, order them to more wholefome rooms till they recover.

A prifoner of rank, a very fenfible man, to whom I was fpeaking concerning gaolers, faid, " They pay nothing to " the crown, and their revenue is not fmall; at the *Con-* " *ciergerie,* it is about fifteen thoufand *livres;* at the *Grand* " *Chatelet,* twenty thoufand; at *Fort L'Eveque,* twenty " thoufand; at the *Petit Chatelet,* twelve thoufand; at " *L'Abbaye,* ten thoufand. And all things confidered," he added, " prifoners have no juft reafon to complain of " this clafs of men in France."

The

The nomination of a gaoler belongs to the magistrates. When he has been nominated, he is proposed to the *procureur general*; and if, after a careful enquiry into his character, it appears that he has the reputation of a man of probity, he is fixed in the office, and takes an oath of fidelity. The office is freely given him without any expence whatever; so that keepers are not tempted, by paying for their places, to opprefs their prifoners. To remove all pretext for fo doing, rents which they formerly paid to the crown are remitted, and the leafes given up.

As for *debtors*, their number is fmall. Of the 202 prifoners in the *Conciergerie*, but fix were *debtors*. In fome other prifons there were a few more. This perhaps is owing to the following good *arrets*. Every bailiff who arrefts and imprifons a *debtor*, muft pay to the gaoler in advance, a month's aliment or fubfiftance, i. e. ten *livres* ten *fous*, equal to nine fhillings Englifh (provifions being at Paris cheaper in general than at London): And if the like fum be not paid within fourteen days after the end of every month, the prifoner is fet at liberty. Befides this, the *debtor* pays no cofts of arrefts, &c. The whole of them falls on the creditor: And fo do all expences occafioned by his ficknefs or death.

As the beft regulations are liable to be abufed, prifoners are not thought fufficiently provided for by *enacting* good laws. The *execution* of them is carefully attended to. The fubftitutes of the *attorney-general* fhould vifit the prifons once a week, to enquire if the rules be obferved; to hear complaints of prifoners; to fee if the fick be properly attended; and the like.—Befides this, the *parliament of Paris* fends to all the prifons five times a year two or three *councellors* with a *fubftitute* of the *attorney general*, and two clerks. They go at Chriftmas, Eafter, Whitfuntide, one
day

day before 15th Auguſt, St Simon and Jude. There is in each priſon (as in other foreign gaols) a room for their reception, called the *council-chamber*. It is occupied at other times by the head gaoler.

The arrival of this deputation is announced by boys, who, though offenders, are allowed to do little errands in the priſon : Theſe go round the court and into every room, giving notice of it aloud. The deputies go, without the gaoler or turnkeys, into every room and dungeon, and,

1ſt. They aſk the priſoners one by one, if they have any complaint to make of the gaoler or his ſervants. But they never meddle with thoſe who are confined by an order from the king.

2. They receive the petitions of criminals who have been detained too long without trial.

3. In caſe of debts not exceeding two thouſand *livres* (about ninety pounds) if the debtor can raiſe a third part of his debt, and no more, they receive it for the creditors. How they clear him of the remaining two thirds, I will ſhew preſently. They take notes of theſe matters in the priſon ; and give an account of all to the parliament, at their general public meeting a day or two after.

In behalf of criminals who have not been tried, the parliament commonly orders the attorney-general to write in their name to the inferior judges, enquiring into the cauſes of delay, or ordering expedition. If a priſoner be acquitted, he is diſcharged within twenty-four hours.

The laws of France do not in ordinary caſes admit a *debtor* to bail without the conſent of his *creditor*. But in

the

the cafe mentioned above, the parliament obliges creditors to accept of bails for the remainder of debts under two thoufand *livres*. And even this bail feems a matter of mere form; for they fometimes take for bail men that are infolvent. I have heard there is no ftanding law for this; and that it is rather an immemorial cuftom: Be.aufe the parliament enacts a particular law for each cafe as it occurs In France there are no infolvent acts.—When prifoners have received their liberty from the king, or their creditors, they cannot be detained a moment for fees, hire of rooms, debts contracted in prifon, or on any pretence whatever.

The deputies hear no complaints of the gaoler againft his prifoners. When he has any to make, he applies to the chief juftice, by whofe order the prifoner was committed. If he was imprifoned by an order from the king, he applies to the lieutenant-general of the police; if without fuch an order, to the lieutenant-criminal, &c.

Befides the deputation now mentioned, the parliament appoints to each prifon one of their own body, a councellor. They always choofe a gentleman of fortune and good character He is called *Commiffaire de la Prifon*. His bufinefs is much like that of the deputation; and his office perpetual. By frequent difcourfe with prifoners I learned, that thefe officers are very humane to the diftreffed. They can (as the parliament) oblige creditors to accept one third part of debts under two thoufand *livres:* But they ufe this power with much caution.

The *Bicetre* is upon a fmall eminence about two miles from Paris. If it were only a prifon, I fhould call it an enormous one; but this for men, like the *Salpetriere* for women, is indeed a kind of general hofpital. Of about four thoufand men that are within its walls, not one half

are

are prifoners. The majority are; the *poor*, who wear a coarfe brown uniform, and feem as miferable as the poor in fome of our country work-houfes: The *infane*: And thofe that have the venereal difcafe. Each fort was in a court and apartments totally feparate from the other, and from *criminals*.

There are two large rooms called *La Force*, on the other fide of the court *(La Cour Royale)* which are crowded with prifoners: In 1778, there were upwards of two hundred. Such a number confined together in idlenefs, muft produce a great corruption of manners. Many at their unhappy end have afcribed their ruin to the flagitious examples they had *here* feen, and the inftructions *here* given them.

The *Baftile* may occur to fome of my readers, as an object concerning which fome information would be acceptable. I am happy to be able to give this, by means of a pamphlet publifhed in 1774, written by a perfon who was long confined in this prifon. It is reckoned the beft account of this celebrated ftructure ever publifhed; and the fale of it being prohibited in France under very fevere penalties, it is become extremely fcarce.

" This caftle is a ftate prifon, confifting of eight very ftrong towers, furrounded with a *fofse* about one hundred and twenty feet wide, and a wall fixty feet high. The entrance is at the end of the ftreet of St Antoine, by a drawbridge and great gates into the court of *L' Hotel du Gouvernment*; and from thence over another draw-bridge to the *corps de garde*, which is feparated by a ftrong barrier conftructed with beams plated with iron, from the great court. This court is one hundred and twenty feet by eighty. In it is a fountain; and fix of the towers furround it, it, which are united by walls of free-ftone ten feet thick up to the top. At the bottom of this court is a large modern *corps de logis*, which feparates it from the court *du Puits*. This court is fifty feet by twenty-five. Contiguous to it, are the other two towers. On the top of the towers is a platform continued in terraces, on which the prifoners are fometimes permitted to walk, attended by a guard. On this platform are thirteen cannons mounted, which are difcharged on days of rejoicing. In the *corps de logis* is the council-chamber, and the kitchen, offices, &c. above thefe are rooms for prifoners of diftinction, and over the council-chamber the king's lieutenant refides. In the court *du Puits* is a large well for the ufe of the kitchen.

" The dungeons of the tower *de Liberte* extend under the kitchen, &c. Near that tower is a fmall chapel on the ground floor. In the wall of it are five nitches or clofets, in which prifoners are put one by one to hear mafs, where they can neither fee nor be feen.

" The dungeons at the bottom of the towers exhale the moft offenfive fcents, and are the recepticles of toads, rats, and other kinds of vermin. In the corner of each is a camp-bed, made of planks laid on iron bars that are fixed to the walls, and the prifoners are allowed fome ftraw to lay on the beds. Thefe dens are dark, having no windows, but openings into the ditch : they have double doors, the inner ones plated with iron, with large bolts and locks.

" Of the five claffes of chambers, the moft horrid next to the dungeons are thofe in which are *cages of iron*. There are three of them. They are formed of beams with ftrong plates of iron, and are each eight feet by fix.

G

" The

" The *calottes*, chambers at the top of the towers, are somewhat more tolerable. They are formed of eight arcades of freestone. Here one cannot walk but in the middle of the room. There is hardly sufficient space for a bed from one arcade to another. The windows, being in walls ten feet thick, and having iron gates within and without, admit but little light. In these rooms the heat is excessive in summer, and the cold in winter. They have stoves.

" Almost all the other rooms (of the towers) are octagons, about twenty feet in diameter, and from fourteen to fifteen high. They are very cold and damp. Each is furnished with a bed of green serge, &c. All the chambers are numbered. The prisoners are called by the name of their tower joined to the number of their room.

" A surgeon and three chaplains reside in the castle. If prisoners of note are dangerously ill, they are generally removed, that they may not die in this prison.—The prisoners who die there are buried in the parish of St Paul, under the name of domestics.

" A library was founded by a prisoner who was a foreigner, and died in the *Bastille* the beginning of the present century. Some prisoners obtain permission to have the use of it.

" One of the centinels on the inside of the castle rings a bell every hour, day and night, to give notice that they are awake: And on the *rounds* on the outside of the castle they ring every quarter of an hour."

I have inserted so particular an account of this prison, chiefly with the design of inculcating a reverence for the principles of a *free constitution* like our own, which will not

permit,

permit, in any degree, the exercife of that defpotifm, which has rendered the name of the *Baftille* fo formidable. I was defirous of examining it myfelf; and for that purpofe knocked hard at the outer gate, and immediately went forward through the guard to the draw-bridge before the entrance of the caftle. But whilft I was contemplating this gloomy manfion, an officer came out much furprifed; and I was forced to retreat through the mute guard, and thus regained that freedom, which for one locked up within thofe walls it is next to impoffible to obtain.

In the *provincial gaols* I faw little worth noting, but what has been already mentioned at Paris. Thefe alfo have five charitable patroneffes, or patrons, who take care that the prifoners be not defrauded of their allowance; and procure them farther relief.

In the prifon at DUNKIRK, the French prifoners were in two or three rooms by themfelves.

Here I found many of my countrymen prifoners of war. In five rooms there were a hundred and thirty-three—*captains, mates, paffengers,* and common failors all crowded together—who lay on ftraw, with one coverlet for every three perfons. In three other rooms there were thirteen accommodated in a better manner, becaufe moft of them were *ranfomers,* and capable of paying fix *fous* a night for their beds. The court was fmall, being only forty-two feet by twenty-fix; nor was there fufficient plenty of water. The bread, beer, and foup were good, and the beef tolerable. Each room was fupplied with two fmall faggots a day for firing. The fick (of whom there were only

G 2 three)

---

* A *ranfomer* is a perfon confined as a fecurity, till the fum is paid for which a fhip has been *ranfomed*.

three) were taken to the military hofpital, and great attention was paid to them.

The common prifon at CALAIS, being fmaller than that
at Dunkirk, was much crowded; for it contained one hundred and twenty-feven Englifh prifoners. Seventeen failors lay in one room* on ftraw, without coverlets; a few
had not even ftraw: On my complaining of this to the *com-
miffary.* he faid, he would fend to St Omer's for coverlets.
After informing him farther, that I had found *captains, paffengers,* and *mates* confined in France, but what I fuppofed
perfons of this defcription in England were on their *parole
of honour;* he replied, and defired I would note it down,
that " a *parole* could not be granted without fecurity; a
" hundred guineas for captains, feventy-five for mates,
" fixty for failors, and twenty-five for boys." Paffengers,
I afterwards learned, were on the fame footing with captains.

S C O T C H AND I R I S H   P R I S O N S.

IT may not be improper, before I enter on a particular
account of Englifh prifons, to mention what further occur-
red to me that feemed worthy of obfervation, in a journey
into Scotland and Ireland in the fummer, 1779.

The prifons which I faw in Edinburgh, Glafgow, Perth,
Stirling, Jedburgh, Air, &c. were old buildings, dirty and
offenfive, without courts, and alfo generally without water. They are not vifited by the magiftrates: And the
gaolers are allowed the fale of the moft pernicious liquors.

If

---

* That room was nineteen feet by twelve. In another fmaller room, in
two tiers, were twenty-three hammocks belonging to the failors; for fometimes their hammocks were given them. The court of this prifon was only
twenty-five feet by fourteen and a half.

If a prisoner for debt declares upon oath that he has not wherewithal to maintain himself, the creditor must aliment him within ten days after such notice is given for that purpose, with at least three-pence a day, but generally the magistrates order six-pence.—By the procefs of *ceffio bonorum*, a debtor, after being a' month in prifon, may obtain his liberty, and be fecured againft execution for any previous debts, by making a furrender of all his effects to be divided among his creditors: Though if he afterwards comes into better circumftances, his effects may be attached for the payment of thofe debts. This compaffionate law prevents a creditor putting his debtor in prifon, unlefs he has good reafon to believe he is acting fraudulently.

Perjury is not frequent in Scotland. The oath, and the form of adminiftering it, are very folemn. The witnefs, holding up his right hand, repeats the following words after the judge:—" By God himfelf, and as you fhall an-" fwer to God at the great day of judgment, you fhall de-" clare the truth, and nothing but the truth, in fo far as " you know, or fhall be afked at you."—The depofitions are read over by the clerk, and figned by the witneffes and the judge.—It is enacted by the twentieth of George II. that " the circuit-courts fhall be regularly held twice in " every year, within that part of Great-Britain called " Scotland, and the judges thereof fhall continue by the " fpace of fix days at the leaft, at each town or place where " the circuit-courts fhall be he held, for the difpatch of " bufinefs."

In the Tolbooth at EDINBURGH,[*] July 6, 1779, there were thirteen debtors and nine felons; and in the Canongate Tolbooth, there were five debtors and one felon: And in

---

[*] I here give the table of fees from the Tolbooth in this city, which is the only one I faw in the prifons in Scotland.

in the *houfe of correction* there were fifty-three women, crowded into dirty and offenfive rooms.

In

ACT of COUNCIL regulating the fees payable to the jailor and clerk of the Tolbooth of Edinburgh.—Edinburgh, 17 July, 1728. The which day the lord provoft, bailies, council, deacons of crafts, ordinary and extraordinary, being convened in council, and taking into confideration the prefent ftate of their Tolbooth, and particularly the fees that have been in ufe to be exacted by the jailor and clerk of the faid prifon, both from creditors at incarceration of prifoners, and from the debtor or perfon himfelf imprifoned; and judging it highly reafonable, that thefe fees fhould for the future be publicly afcertained by authority of the council for the benefit of all concerned; therefore the council do tax and fettle the fame as follows, *viz.*

FEES *payable to the* JAILOR.

The incarcerator of any debitor for any fum of money fhall pay at incarceration one halfpenny fterling for each pound *Scots*, and another halfpenny fterling of each pound *Scots* to be paid by the debitor at his liberation; and this in place of one penny fterling of each pound *Scots* in ufe to be paid by creditors at incarceration, and of the like fum of one penny fterling of each pound *Scots*, ufually paid by the debitor at liberation as relief money.

	Scots $\pounds$. *s.* *d.*
Item, Each perfon imprifoned for a civil debt or otherwife not being a burgefs, fhall pay to the jailor of houfe dues each night attour what is above — — —	0 ·6 8
Item, Each burgefs imprifoned for a civil debt or otherwife, fhall pay alfo to the gaoler of houfe dues each night attour what is above	0 3 4
Item, The incarcerator of any perfon or perfons by the lord's letters of laburrows fhall pay at incarceration — —	3 0 0
Item, The incarcerator of any perfon or perfons on laburrows by a magiftrate, fheriff, or juftice of peace, fhall pay at incarceration	1 10 0
Item, The incarcerator of any perfon for exhibition of papers, or for implementing of writs (captions for reproductions of proceffes before the inferior courts excepted) fhall pay at an incarceration	1 10 0

The council ordains and declares when any gentleman or other perfon fhall be incarcerate in the Tolbooth, and fhall defire to have a room in the prifon by him or herfelf, fuch perfons fhall be liable, for the conveniency of fuch room, to pay to the jailor ten fhillings fterling weekly in place of prifon fees, or fuch as they and the jailor fhall agree, but not to exceed ten fhillings.

That all prifoners fhall be liable to pay the under-keepers, and the woman who cleans the houfe, as prifoners were in ufe to do before the act of council, the 17th day of July 1728; but if any difpute fhall arife thereanent, the the magiftrates for the time being fhall have the full power of determining the fame.

The

In the Tolpooth at GLASGOW, July 9, 1779, there were thirteen debtors and seven felons; and in the *houfe of correction,* feventeen women were fpinning, decently clothed.

IRE-

Fees *payable to the* Clerk *of the* Tolbooth.

	Scots.
	£. s. d.

Imprimis, Each perfon incarcerate upon any laburrows, fhall at his liberation pay   —   —   —   0 12 0

Item, Each perfon incarcerate by warrant from the magiftrates, fhall at his liberation pay   —   —   —   0 6 0

Item, Each perfon incarcerate by warrant from fheriff or juftice of the peace, fhall at liberation pay   —   —   0 12 0

Item, All government prifoners fhall pay each at liberation   2 0 0

Item, For each petition by a prifoner for the benefit of the act of grace, and for the clerk's declaration thereto fubjoined fhall be paid   —   —   —   —   0 6 0

Item, For the borrowing or delivery up of any deligence by which prifoners are incarcerate (all magiftrates' warrants at or within ten mercks excepted) fhall be paid   —   —   0 4 0

Item, All perfons incarcerated or arrefted for a fum or fums at or below £.120 *Scots,* fhall pay to the clerk at liberation four pennies for each pound *Scots*; and for fums above £.120 *Scots,* fhall pay at liberation to the clerk two pound *Scots* and no more

Item, All perfons incarcerate for exhibition of papers, or for implementing of writs (captions for reproduction of proceffes before the inferior courts excepted) fhall pay to the clerk at liberation   1 10 0

Item, All creditors or incarcerators of prifoners for civil debt or otherwife fhall be free of all fees to the clerk at incarceration

And the council ftatues and declares, that if any fees fhall be demanded or exacted in time coming, by the jailor or clerk of their Tolbooth, other than thefe above fet down, they fhall incur the deprivation of their refpective offices; and ordain their prefents to be printed and publifhed, that none may pretend ignorance.

And the council hereby ordains James Cleland, principal jailor, and his fucceffors in office, to affix a copy hereof in the Tolbooth-hall, and in his own office, under the penalty of £.5 *Scots, toties quoties.*

Extracted (figned) GEORGE HOME.

Edinburgh, the fixth day of July, feventeen hundred and feventy-nine years. Thefe do certify by me William Gilles, clerk to the Tolbooth of Edinburgh, that the above is a true and exact copy of the act of council of the city of Edinburgh, by which the keeper of the faid Tolbooth and me as clerk thereof are governed.

WILLIAM GILLES.

I R E L A N D.

I was happy in finding at DUBLIN a new gaol (New-gate) almoſt ready for the removal of the priſoners into more airy and convenient apartments, in which the ſhock-ing intercourſe of the two ſexes which took place in the old priſon, will be avoided. This new priſon is one hun-dred and ſeventy feet in length, and has ſeparate courts for men and women. The cells on the firſt and ſecond floors are about twelve feet by eight, and on the upper floor twelve by four, all arched with brick, to prevent danger from fire. I chuſe to ſay nothing of the under-ground dungeons, for I hope they will never be uſed. It might be beſt to convert the chapel at the top of the houſe into an infirmary; for the ſick rooms are too ſmall, and likely to produce infection.

In the men's court there is a pump which ſupplies good water, and I ſuppoſe the women's court will be provided with another. Great attention ſhould be paid to air and cleanlineſs in the ſtaircaſes, and the narrow paſſages lead-ing to the cells, to prevent them from becoming offenſive and infectious.

The criminals in the gaols of Ireland are very numerous; one reaſon of which may be, that in this country there are no houſes of correction; and another, that acquitted per-ſons are continued in confinement till they have diſchar-ged their fees to the clerk of the crown, or peace, the ſhe-riff, gaoler and turnkey. Even boys almoſt naked, and under the age of twelve, are ſometimes confined two years for theſe fees, though amounting to no more than about forty ſhillings. How ſurpriſing is it, that any kingdom can endure ſuch injuſtice! It is a particular aggravation

of

of it, that the prisoners thus confined generally lose, at the same time, their allowance of bread. I have heard that Mr Justice Aston always ordered the acquitted prisoners to be discharged.—Some boys were lately released from the county gaol at Kilmainham, paying half fees; and others from Newgate, the sheriffs of Dublin geneously relinquishing their fees. But as those boys had been associated with the most profligate and abandoned felons for many months, I did not in the least wonder to find that some of them returned to their former habitation in a few days.

A PARTICULAR ACCOUNT of ENGLISH PRISONS.

As the Tables of which the present Account will chiefly consist, contain several terms which cannot be familiar to the generality of my readers, I shall begin with an explanation of them.

In the first page of every county, city, &c. the second article of the *gaoler* or *keeper*'s emolument is *fees;* by which are meant such only as are taken by him and his servants on the admission or discharge of a prisoner. The sums set down against this article are from the best information I could procure in my repeated journeys; but they differ sometimes from those specified in the *tables of fees.*

Wherever there were *tables of fees,* I thought myself obliged to give exact and literal copies of them: I am not therefore answerable for the improprieties of expression, or defects of form to be found in some of them: But to prevent

H

vent tirefome and ufelefs repetitions, I have abridged the formalities of preamble and conclufion.*

The T O W E R.

This is a ftrong fortrefs, and the only prifon in *England* for ftate delinquents of rank. The care of it is committed to an officer called the *Conftable* of the Tower, who has under him a lieutenant, deputy-lieutenant called the *governor*, and many other officers, among whom are forty *warders*, whofe uniform is the fame with the king's yeoman of the guards. Nineteen of thefe warders have feparate houfes well furnifhed, in any of which, as the governor is pleafed to order, the ftate delinquents may be confined; and the cuftom has been to affign them two of the beft rooms on the firft floor. Sometimes they are committed to clofe confinement; but in general they are at liberty to walk in the area of the tower, attended always with a warder.

There have been no prifoners here for a few years paft; and when there are any, there fate is foon determined by a legal trial, and confequently their confinement can never be long. Six fhillings and eight-pence a day is allowed by government for their fubfiftence, but they feldom accept this allowance.

In this fortrefs, befides the houfes juft mentioned, there are feveral public offices and ftore-houfes; fuch, particularly, as the office of Ordnance, the Jewel-office, the Mint, and buildings for holding artillery and arms.

N E W-

It fhould be obferved, that by the ftatute 32 George II. if any gaoler, or keeper, demand fees not fet down in a table figned by the juftices, and afterwards confirmed by the judge or judges of affize, and juftices, and hung up confpicuous in the prifon; fuch demand is illegal, and the offender is liable to a penalty of fifty pounds to the perfon injured.

N E W G A T E.

GAOLER, *Richard Akerman.*
    Salary,   £.200
    Fees,   Debtors, — — £.0 : 8 : 10.
            Felons, — — 0 : 18 : 10.
            Mifdemeanours or Fines, 0 : 14 : 10.
            Tranfports, — — 0 : 14 : 10.
    Licence, Beer and Wine.

PRISONERS,

    Allowance, Debtors, } a penny loaf a day.
               Felons,

    Garnifh, Debtors, £.0 : 5 : 6.
           Felons, &c. 0 : 2 : 6.

Number,	Debtors.	Felons, &c.		Debtors.	Felons, &c.
1775, March 5,	33,	190.	1776, Dec. 26, 33,		152.
1776, —— 1,	38,	129.	1779, Aug. 16, 51,		141.
—— May 17,	46,	212.			

CHAPLAIN, Rev. Mr *Villette.*
    Duty,   Sunday twice; every day prayers;
            once a month facrament.
    Salary, £.35, &c.
SURGEON, Mr *Olney.*
    Salary, £50. for all prifoners.

THE builders of Old Newgate feem to have regarded in their plan, nothing but the fingle article of keeping prifoners in fafe cuftody. The rooms and cells were fo clofe, as to be almoft the conftant feats of difeafe, and fources of infection; to the deftruction of multitudes, not only in the prifon, but abroad. The city had therefore very good reafon for their refolution to build a new gaol. Many inconveniencies of the old gaol are avoided in the new one: But it has fome manifeft errors. It is now too late to point out particulars. All I will fay, is, that without more than ordinary care, the prifoners in it will be in great danger of the gaol fever.

The cells built in Old Newgate a few years fince for
              con-

condemned malefactors, are intended for the fame ufe at
prefent. I fhall therefore give fome account of them. There
are, upon each of the three floors, five; all vaulted, near
nine feet high to the crown. Thofe on the ground floor
meafure full nine feet by near fix; the five on the firft
ftory are a little larger, on account of the fet-off in the wall;
and the five uppermoft, ftill a little larger for the fame reafon. In the upper part of each cell, is a window double
grated, near three feet by one and a half. The doors are
four inches thick. The ftrong ftone wall is lined all round
each cell with planks, ftudded with broad-headed nails.
In each cell is a barrack bedftead. I was told by thofe
who attended me, that criminals who had affected an air of
boldnefs during their trial, and appeared quite unconcern-
ed at the pronouncing fentence upon them, were ftruck
with horror, and fhed tears, when brought to thefe dark-
fome folitary abodes.

The new chapel is plain and neat. Below are three or
four pews for men-felons, &c. On each fide is a gallery:
That towards the womens' ward is for them: In it is a pew
for the keeper, whofe prefence may fet a good example,
and be otherwife ufeful. The other gallery towards the
debtors' ward is for them. The ftairs to each gallery are
on the outfide of the chapel. I went twice to prayers
there. Mr Villette read them diftinctly, and with propriety: The few prifoners who were prefent, feemed attentive; but we were difturbed by the noife in the court.
Surely they who will not go to chapel, who are by far the
greater number, fhould be locked up in their rooms during
the time of divine fervice, aud not fuffered to hinder the
edification of fuch as are better difpofed.

The *chaplain* (or *ordinary*) befides his falary, has a
houfe in Newgate-ftreet, clear of land-tax; two freedoms
yearly,

yearly, which commonly fell for £.25 each; lady Barnadif-
ton's legacy, £.6 a year; an old legacy paid by the gover-
nors of St Bartholomew's hofpital, £.10 pounds a year; the
city generally prefents him once in fix months with another
freedom. He engages when chofen to hold no other living.

Debtors have every Saturday from the chamber of London eight ftone of beef: *Fines* four ftone: And fome years
felons eight ftone. Debtors have feveral legacies. I inquired for a lift of them, and Mr Akerman told me the
table in Maitland's *Survey* was authentic. The amount of
it is £.52 : 5 : 8 a year. There are other donations
mentioned by Maitland, amounting to fixty-four ftone of
beef, and five dozen of bread.

To thefe he adds the donation of " Robert Dow, who
left £.1 : 6 : 8 yearly for ever to the fexton or bellman
of St Sepulchre's, to pronounce folemnly two exhortations
to the perfons condemned, the night before their execution; in thefe words,

You prifoners who are within
Who for wickednefs and fin,

after many mercies fhewn you, are now appointed to die
to-morrow in the forenoon, give ear and underftan dthat
to-morrow morning the greateft bell of St Sepulchre'sfhall
toll for you in form and manner of a paffing bell as ufed
to be tolled for thofe that are at the point of death, to the
end that all godly people may pray, &c. &c.

T A B L E of F E E S.

London fc. A *Table* of *Fees* to be taken by the Gaoler or Keeper of Newgate within the faid City of London for any Prifoner or Prifoners committed or coming into Gaol or Chamber-Rent there or difcharge from thence in
any *Civil Action* fettled and eftablifhed the nineteenth day of December in
the

the third year of the reign of his Majefty King George the Second *Annoque Domini* 1729 purfuant to an Act of Parliament lately made intituled **An Act** for the Relief of *Debtors* with refpect to the imprifonment of their perfons.

	£.	s.	d.
Every prifoner on the mafter-fide fhall pay to the keeper for his entrance fee	0	3	0
Every prifoner on the mafter-fide fhall pay for chamber-room ufe of bed bedding and fheets to the keeper there being two in a bed and no more each *per* week	0	1	3
Every prifoner on the faid mafter-fide who at his own defire fhall have a bed to himfelf, fhall pay to the keeper for chamber-room ufe of bed bedding and fheets *per* week	0	2	6
Every debtor fhall pay to the keeper for his difcharging fee	0	6	10

And to all the turnkeys two fhillings and no more
No other fee for the ufe of chamber bed bedding or fheets or upon the commitments or difcharge of any prifoner on any civil action.

H I S   M A J E S T Y's   P R I S O N.

T H E   F L E E T, for D E B T O R S.

WARDEN, *John Eyles*, Efq.
  Deputy Warden and Clerk of the Papers,
    Daniel Hopkins, now *William Lowe*,
  Salary,
  Fees,   £. 1 : 6 : 8   } on entrance, *per* account
           0 : 2 : 0   Turnkey,   } from the prifoners.
  Licence,   Beer and Wine to *John Cartwright*, now—*Hall*, who
    holds of the warden on leafe the tap &c.

PRISONERS.
  Allowance, none.
  Garnifh, £. 0 : 2 : 0
  Number,   —   In the Houfe.   In the Rules.
    1774, April 26,   171,   — —   71.
    1776, —— 2,   241,   — —   78.
    1779, Aug. 13,   147,   — —   37.
CHAPLAIN, Rev. Mr *Holmer.*

  Duty,   Sunday twice; Wednefday prayers.
  Salary
SURGEON, None.

To this prifon were committed formerly thofe who incurred the difpleafure of the Star-chamber. In the 16th of
                                    Charles

Charles I. when that court was abolifhed, it became a prifon for debtors, and for perfons charged with contempts
of the courts of chancery, exchequer, and common pleas.

In 1728, many abufes practifed by the warden were the
fubject of parliamentary inquiry.

The prifon was rebuilt a few years fince. At the front
is a narrow court. At each end of the building, there is
a fmall projection or wing. There are four floors, they
call them *galleries*, befides the cellar-floor, called *Bartho-
lomew-Fair*. Each gallery confifts of a paffage in the middle, the whole length of the prifon, 66 yards ; and rooms
on each fide of it about 14½ feet by 12½, and 9½ high. A
chimney and window in every room. The paffages are
narrow (not feven feet wide) and darkifh, having only a
window at each end. On the firft floor, the *hall gallery*, to
which you afcend by eight fteps, are, a chapel, a tap-room
—a coffee-room (lately made out of two rooms for debtors), a room for the turnkey, another for the watchman,
and eighteen rooms for prifoners. Befides the coffee-room
and tap-room, two of thofe eighteen rooms, and all the cellar floor, except a lock up room to confine the diforderly,
and another room for the turnkey, were held by the tapfter,
John Cartwright, who bought the remainder of the leafe
at public auction in 1775. The cellar floor is fixteen
fteps below the hall-gallery. It confifts of the two rooms juft
now mentioned, the tapfter's kitchen, his four large beer
and wine cellars, and fifteen rooms for prifoners. Thefe fifteen, and the two before mentioned on the hall gallery, the
tapfter lets to prifoners for from four to eight fhillings a
week.

On the *firft gallery* (that next above the hall-gallery) are
twen-

twenty-five rooms for prisoners. On the *second gallery*
twenty-seven : One of them, fronting the staircase, is their
committee-room. A room at one end is an infirmary.
At the other end, in a large room over the chapel, is a dirty billiard-table ; kept by the prisoner who sleeps in that
room. On the highest story are twenty-seven rooms.
Some of these upper rooms, *viz.* those in the wings, are
larger than the rest ; being over the chapel, the tap-room,
&c. All the rooms I have mentioned are for master's-side
debtors. The weekly rent of those not held by the tapster is 1*s*. 3*d*. unfurnished. They fall to the prisoners in
succession, thus : When a room becomes vacant, the first
prisoner upon the list of such as have paid their entrance-
fees, takes possession of it. When the prison was built, the
warden gave each prisoner his choice of a room according
to his seniority as prisoner. If all of them be occupied,
a new comer must hire of some tenant a part of his room ;
or shift as he can. Prisoners are excluded from all right
of succession to the rooms held by the tapster, and let at
the high rents aforesaid. The apartments for common-
side debtors are only part of the right wing of the prison.
Besides the cellar (which was intended for their kitchen,
but is occupied with lumber, and shut up) there are four
floors. On each floor is a room about 24 or 25 feet
square, with a fire-place ; and on the sides, seven closets
or cabins to sleep in. Such of these prisoners as swear in
court or before a commissioner that they are not worth five
pounds, and cannot subsist without charity (of them there
were at one of my visits sixteen, at other times not so
many) have the donations which are sent to the prison,
the begging-box and the grate.

There is plenty of water from the river and pumps ; and
a spacious court behind the prison.

I

I mentioned the billiard-table. They alſo play in the court at ſkittles, miſſiſippi, fives, tennis &c. And not only the priſoners: I ſaw among them ſeveral butchers and others from the market; who are admitted here as at another public houſe. The ſame may be ſeen in many other priſons where the gaoler keeps or lets the tap. Beſides the inconvenience of this to priſoners; the frequenting a priſon leſſens the dread of being confined in one. On Monday night there was a wine-club: On Thurſday night a beer-club: Each laſting uſually till one or two in the morning. I need not ſay how much riot theſe occaſion; and how the ſober priſoners, and thoſe that are ſick, are annoyed by them.

Seeing the priſon crowded with women and children, I procured an accurate liſt of them; and found that on (or about) the 6th of April 1776, when there were on the maſter's-ſide 213 priſoners, on the common-ſide 30, total 243; their wives (including women of an appellation not ſo honourable) and children were 475.

N E W   L U D G A T E.

This priſon for debtors who are free of the city, for clergymen, proctors and attorneys, was formerly a bride-well to the London work-houſe adjoining.

On the ground floor are, a long-room, a tap-room, and a kitchen. In each of them is a ſtaircaſe; leading firſt to eleven rooms for maſter's-ſide debtors—viz. over the long-room, a ſizeable chamber, and a room on each of the two floors above: Over the tap-room, four ſmall rooms, which have iron bars at the windows, and a large room above them: Over the kitchen, a ſizeable chamber, and two rooms above. The common-ſide debtors are in two large

I

gar-

garrets, the *Foreſt* and *Dock*. The priſon is out of repair. No regard has been paid to the act, which enjoins white-waſhing, &c. A ſmall court, with a ciſtern for river-water. No infirmary. The chapel is common to the priſon and work-houſe. Chaplain, Rev. Mr *Henry Foulkes*.

The city allowance is ten ſtone of beef a week: To which has been added ſince the 9th of February, 1776, a penny loaf a day for each priſoner. The lord mayor and ſheriffs ſend annually coals: And Meſſrs Calvert and Co formerly ſent from the Peacock brewhouſe weekly a generous donation of two barrels of ſmall beer. Keeper's ſalary, £70: Fees, fee table. He lives diſtant; but the deputy is conſtant and careful in his attendance, and reſpected by the priſoners.

I found the priſon very clean. The tap is ſhut at ten every night. On Sunday, a board is placed at the gate, on which is painted, " No admittance from 10 o'clock to 12, nor from 2 to 4."

A T A B L E of F E E S
To be taken by the Keeper of his Majeſty's Priſon of Ludgate.

	£.	s.	d.
Every priſoner ſhall pay at his or her coming in — —	0	1	0
Every priſoner ſhall pay for chamber-room, bed, bedding and ſheets, in the beſt ſide called the maſter-ſide, being two in a bed, each *per* week. — — —	0	1	0
Every priſoner on the ſecond lodging called the common ſide, ſhall pay for uſe of chamber-rent, bed, bedding, and ſheets, two in a bed and no more, each *per* night — —	0	0	1½
Every priſoner who at his own deſire ſhall have a bed to himſelf in any of the beſt rooms called the maſter-ſide, ſhall pay for bed, bedding, and ſheets *per* week — —	0	2	6
Every priſoner who at his own deſire has a bed to himſelf in the ſecond lodging or common ſide, ſhall pay for chamber-room, bed, bedding, and ſheets *per* night — —	0	0	3
Every priſoner in the meaneſt ward, who at his own deſire hath a bed to himſelf, ſhall pay for the uſe of bedding, &c. *per* night	0	0	2

Every

£. s. d.

Every prifoner in the meaneft ward, two in a bed and no more, for
the ufe of the bed, bedding, &c. *per* night — 0 0 1
If the prifoners find their own bedding (which the keeper fhall in no
wife hinder) then they fhall pay for chamber-room, if more beds
than one in a room, each *per* week — — 0 0 3
If the prifoner hath a room to himfelf, and provide himfelf with bed
and bedding, which the keeper is in no fort to hinder him of,
then he fhall pay for chamber-room *per* week — 0 0 4
The prifoners' inability to find a couch, and to pay *per* week 0 0 1

P O U L T R Y C O M P T E R.

KEEPER, *Chriftopher Hayes*, who purchafed of the city for life, and
has let it *now* to *Henry Weft*.
Salary, none.
Fees, Debtors, £0 : 15 : 8.
Felons, 0 : 13 : 4.
Tranfports, taken from the Old Bailey by Mr Akerman.
Licence, Beer and Wine. Tap let.

PRISONERS,
Allowance, Debtors a penny loaf a day.
Felons, a penny loaf a day.
Garnifh, Debtors, £0 : 4 : 8. It is called ward-dues for
Felons, 0 : 1 : 6. candles, &c.

CHAPLAIN, Rev Dr *Trufler*.
Duty, Every other Sunday evening.
Salary, £30.
SURGEON, None.

For mafter's fide debtors there are about fifteen rooms
between the inner and outer gates. For common fide
debtors, fix wards within the inner gate, two of them on
the ground floor, *viz.* the *King's Ward*, in which (1776)
were 24 debtors; and the *Prince's Ward*, 9 debtors. Above
thofe wards are the *Middle Ward*, in it were 20 debtors;
and the *Women's Ward*, 2 debtors. Above them are the
Upper Ward, 11 debtors; and the *Jews Ward*, 4 Jew
debtors. Near the middle ward, on the fame floor, is a
clofe darkifh room for the fick. In each ward, a fire-
place. The rooms are out of repair: But the debtors
keep their floors very clean. The court is fmall, but that
alfo is clean: The water conftantly running.

I 2 The

The tap-room is in the court. Adjoining is the felons' day-room, the *Bell*. Their night-rooms, one for men, another for women, are up ftairs. But the womens' room was occupied for a work-fhop by a prifoner, a cooper; and the women flept in the *Bell* below. No ftraw or bedding.

On one fide of the court is a chapel; with a narrow gallery all round for mafter's-fide debtors. The chapel, and indeed the whole of the prifon, is quite out of repair.

At the roof of the prifon, are fpacious leads, on which the mafter's-fide debtors are fometimes allowed to walk: But then the keeper is with them: For the leads communicate with the adjoining houfes, one of which affords a ready efcape from fo clofe a prifon in cafe of fire.

Befides the penny loaf a day, which is from the chamber of London, there are fome legacies to the debtors paid by the companies in this city, amounting to about £.60 a year: They have alfo from the fheriffs 32 pounds of beef on Saturdays, and they had formerly from the Peacock brewhoufe (Meffis Calvert and Co.) a kind donation of two barrels of fmall beer a week.

In this prifon 8 men in 1776 had with them their wives and 19 children. The other prifoners, I learned, had 44 wives and 144 children, not in the gaol.

The act for preferving the health of prifoners, and the claufes againft fpirituous liquors, are not hung up.

The keeper pays the city £.30 pounds a year rent, which is refunded to him for his trouble on night-charges.

POUL-

POULTRY COMPTER, *viz.*

A Table of Fees taken by the Warden, Gaoler, or Keeper of the Poultry Compter within the city of London for any Prisoners' Commitment or coming into Gaol, or Chamber-Rent there, or Difcharge from thence in any *Civil Action* fettled and eftablifhed the 15th January, in the 3d Year of the Reign of King George II. and in the year of our Lord 1729 purfuant to an Act of Parliament lately made, entitled " An Act for the Relief of Debtors with Refpect to the Imprifonment of their Perfons."

	£.	s.	d.
Every prifoner who at his own defire fhall go into the beft ward on the mafter's-fide fhall pay to the keeper for his entrance fee	0	3	0
To the turnkeys for fuch entrance — —	0	1	0
Every prifoner in the beft ward on the mafter's-fide to pay to the keeper for his difcharging fee — —	0	6	10
To the turnkeys upon fuch difcharge —	0	1	0
Every fuch prifoner in the beft ward on the mafter-fide, who at his own defire fhall have a bed to himfelf, to pay for chamber-room, ufe of bed, bedding, and fheets, to pay to the keeper *per* week	0	2	6
If two in a bed, and no more—for chamber-room, ufe of bed, bedding, and fheets, to pay to the keeper each *per* week	0	1	3
In the fecond ward on the mafter-fide to the keeper for their entrance fee to pay — — —	0	3	0
To the keeper on their difcharge — —	0	6	10
To the turnkeys on fuch difcharge — —	0	2	0
Every fuch prifoner at his own defire fhall have a bed to him or herfelf to pay for chamber, ufe of bed, bedding, and fheets, to pay to the keeper *per* week — —	0	2	4
If two in a bed and no more, to pay for chamber room, ufe of bed, bedding, and fheets, each *per* week — —	0	1	2
In the third ward commonly called the fifteenpenny ward entrance nothing, when difcharged to the keeper —	0	6	0
To the turnkeys on fuch difcharge — —	0	2	0
Every fuch prifoner fhall have at his own defire a bed to him or herfelf, to pay to the keeper for chamber-room, for the ufe of bed, bedding, and fheets, *per* week — —	0	1	3
In the fourth or common ward, for entrance and lodging nothing			
When difcharged to the keeper — —	0	6	0
To the turnkey on fuch difcharge — —	0	2	0

WOOD-STREET COMPTER.

KEEPER, *John Kirby.*
Salary, none.
Fees, Debtors, £0 : 15 : 8.
      Felons, 0 : 11 : 6.
Tranfports, taken from the Old Bailey by Mr Akerman.
Licence, Beer and Wine. Tap let.

PRISONERS,

Allowance, Debtors, } a penny loaf a day.
          Felons,

    Garnish, £0 : 1 : 2.

CHAPLAIN, Rev. Mr *Nash.*
    Duty,   Sunday (conftant).
    Salary,   £50.

SURGEON,   None.

This prifon, built, as appears by infcription on the front, in 1670, has only a fmall court or paffage for all prifoners. Many apartments; yet but two rooms for commonfide debtors: That for the men, which is their day-room, night-room, and kitchen, with a copper, &c is dark and dirty; about 35 feet by 18, and 16 feet high; far too fmall for the number of prifoners, many of whom fleep in 23 beds, which are on three ftories of galleries, or broad fhelves. At one of my vifits there were in this room 39 debtors; feven of them had their wives and children. The room fwarms with bugs. The day and nightroom for women-debtors is more lightfome; in it were only two prifoners Beyond it is a room ruinous, and fit for no ufe.

For men-felons there are two rooms; and two for women; one of thefe is a dark cell. No bedding or ftraw. Thofe who choofe a bed pay 1s. a night; or elfe 10s. 6d. floorage, and 3s. 6d. a week. Near thofe four rooms are twenty-three more for mafter's-fide debtors.

In the court is the chapel; and under it the tap-room, down fixteen fteps. All the rooms aforefaid are within the inner gate; between which and the outer gate (i e. in the keeper's houfe) are more rooms for mafter's-fide debtors.

                                   The

The prifon is greatly out of repair; the main wall on one fide, fhored and propped. No infirmary. The act for preferving the health of prifoners not hung up.

Some years fince, there came once a fortnight to com‑mon-fide debtors in this prifon, nine ftone of beef, and fourteen quartern loaves; and the like relief to other pri‑fons alfo. The charitable hand was concealed; till, the donation failing on the death of the amiable princefs Ca‑roline, it was fuppofed that her highnefs had been the ge‑nerous benefactrefs. And upon reprefenting to the lady who had been almoner to the princefs, the diftrefs of the prifoners, fhe obtained from the late king a renewal of the charity; which was continued during his Majefty's life.

A *Table* of the *Fees* to be paid by the prifoners in *Wood-flreet Compter*.

	£.	s.	d.
For every debtor that hath a room on the mafter-fide, for his or her entrance or floorage — — —	0	5	0
For his or her rent *per* week provided the keeper find bed, bedding, and fheets — — —	0	2	6
If two in one room, to pay weekly each of them —	0	1	3
If a debtor or debtors provide their own bed, bedding, &c. to pay for one or two in one room, weekly for the room —	0	1	3
Exclufive of the Office-Fees { Each debtor on his or her difcharge —	0	8	0
If on the mafter-fide — —	0	8	10
For every debtor in the ward called the fifteenpenny ward—if the keeper provide bed, bedding, and one fheet—weekly	0	1	3
For every debtor on the keeper's-fide, on his or her entrance there, to pay — — — —	0	10	8
For each room—to pay weekly — —	0	2	6
All perfons in any of the charity wards to pay no entrance, or rent			
For every prifoner committed for felony, mifdemeanour or affault on his or her difcharge (except by proclamation at a gaol delive‑ry, then nothing) — — —	0	12	8
For the copy of commitment — —	0	1	6

BRIDE-

B R I D E W E L L.

This building was formerly a palace, near St Bridget's (St Bride's) well; from whence it had the name; which, after it became a prison, was applied to other prisons of the same sort. It was given to the city by King Edward VI. in 1552.

That part of Bridewell which relates to my subject has wards for men and women quite separate.—The men's ward on the ground floor is a day-room, in which they beat hemp; and, down two steps, their night-room. The women's ward is a day-room on the ground floor, in which they beat hemp; and a night-room over it. I was told that the chamber above this is to be fitted up for an infirmary. The sick have, hitherto, been commonly sent to St Bartholomew's hospital. All the prisoners are kept within doors. The women's rooms are large, and have opposite windows, for fresh air. Their ward, as well as the men's, has plenty of water; and their is a hand-ventilator on the outside, with a tube to each room of the women's ward. This is of great service, when the rooms are crowded with prisoners, and the weather is warm.

The prisoners are employed by a hemp-dresser, who has the profit of their labour, an apartment in the prison, and a salary of £13. I generally found them at work; they are provided for, so as to be able to perform it. The hours of work are in winter from eight to four; in summer from six to six, deducting meal-times. The steward is allowed eight-pence a day for the maintenance of each prisoner; and contracts to supply them as follows:---On Sunday, Monday, Tuesday, and Thursday, a penny loaf, ten ounces of dressed beef without bone, broth, and three pints of ten shilling beer: On Wednesday, Friday, and Saturday,

day,

day, a penny loaf, four ounces of cheefe or fome butter, a pint of milk pottage, and three pints of beer. The porter or keeper is now *Thomas Holt*. Salary, £80; no fees. To the women's ward there is a matron, *Sarah Lyon;* falary £60. She takes care of the fick, both men and women, and is allowed a fhilling a day for thofe that are put on the fick diet.

A good regulation has been lately made; every perfon committed a fecond time to this prifon fhall have only half the allowance. A proper check where the allowance is fo ample.

NEW PRISON CLERKENWELL.

GAOLER,   *James Elmore,* now *Samuel Newport.*
   Salary,   £.30, now 70.
   Fees,   £.0 : 7 : 0.
   Tranfports, the expence.
   Licence,   Beer and Wine. The Tap let.

PRISONERS,
   Allowance, a penny loaf a day.
   Garnifh,   £.0 : 1 : 4.

CHAPLAIN,   Rev. Mr *Richards.*
   Duty,   Sunday twice; Tuefday and Thurfday prayers.
   Salary,   £50.

SURGEON,   Mr *Cibbcs.*
   Salary,   £60, for this prifon and the bridewell.

This prifon, built in 1775, is much more commodious than the former of the fame name. Over the gate-way are two rooms, called *Night-Charges,* for prifoners brought in the night to be examined by a magiftrate the next day. (In one of them are keeper's beds.) From that outer gate you pafs on to the gate of the men's court on the right-hand, and of the women's to the left. To each you defcend feven fteps. In the mens' court is a large open fhed,

K   which

which is their day-room. The roof too low for the depth; it has a chimney. Their night-ward, into which they are not permitted to go in the day-time, that the air in it may be cool and fresh, is a house on the other side of the court, divided into two apartments. Each has a room on the ground floor, a chamber, and an upper room. In one part, each of these rooms is 30 feet by 31; in the other, 30 by 20; near ten feet high; well planked all o-ver; no chimneys. For the free circulation of air, every room has in front, to the court, two windows, and back-wards three, with iron bars, and shutters; but, very pro-perly, no glass. Barrack beds in every room; but in each of the two chambers, and in one of the lower rooms, are other beds for those who pay 3s. 6d. a week: When these are occupied, no prisoners sleep on the barrack beds in those rooms. In this court is a lock-up room for the un-ruly. All the stairs are stone.

M I D D L E S E X.

A T A B L E of F E E S

Taken by the Keeper of *New Prison Clerkenwell.*

	£.	s.	d.
For keeping and discharging every person committed by warrant of commitment — — — —	0	6	0
For turning the key at every such person's discharge	0	1	0
For going with any person before a justice —	0	1	0
For a copy of commitment — —	0	1	4

Prisoners brought in by constables of the night, and carried before justices of the peace and discharged, to pay two shillings for his or her discharge.

No spirituous liquors allowed to be brought in here.

KEEPER,   *Edward Hall.*
    Salary,   £50.
    Fees,   £0 : 7 : 0.
    Transports, taken from court by Mr Akerman.
    Licence,   Beer and Wine.   Tap let.

PRISONERS,
    Allowance, a penny loaf a day.
    Garnish, £0 : 1 : 4.

CHAPLAIN,

CHAPLAIN, Rev. Mr *Richards*.

Duty, } *See New Prifon.*
Salary, }

SURGEON, Mr *Gibbes*.
Salary, *See New Prifon.*

Over the gate, two new rooms for night-charges, as at the New Prifon. In the Prifon, men and women have feparate courts and wards. The men have in their court three fheds for day-rooms; one, 6 feet by 16; the other two, 6 by 10 each; full 8 feet high. Their night-rooms oppofite on the ground-floor, one for fines, and one for other offenders, are about 20 feet by 14 each; with barrack beds. One of them was fo crowded, that fome prifoners flept in hammocks. Over thefe night-rooms are chambers with beds for thofe who pay 3s 6d. a week; and another room alfo for fines; joining to which, is a fmall clofe room ufed as an infirmary for men. In another part of the court is a hemp or work-fhop: It is a paffage to fix little work-fhops for faulty apprentices; 7 feet by 3½ each; fronting thefe are their fix night-rooms, larger than the fhops (8 by 4); all on the ground floor.

In the womens' court are three fheds or day-rooms; fame fize as thofe of the men; with a hemp-fhop or work-fhop. Over this, and the men's workfhop, is a long gallery or paffage; on the back of which were twelve dark unwholefome night-rooms for women; 9 feet by 7 each, and 10½ high (in fome of them are beds for thofe who pay): But two of thefe rooms are now made into one for an infirmary for the women.

The keeper pays window-tax; and £2. a year for New-River water; which is directly from the *main*, and always on. Befides this they have good water at a pump in each court.

In July, 1775, the juftices augmented the fees from 5s. 6d to 7s. At the fame time, in *lieu* of fees from acquitted prifoners, which were cancelled by the late act, they paid the keeper at the rate of £20. a year from the time when that act took place.

This prifon is much too fmall for the number committed to it.—At my laft vifit it vas clean.—Of the 171 prifoners.—22 men and boys, and 58 women were convicts. Thefe were employed in picking oakum; the women in in two rooms below, the men up ftairs.* A warehoufe and a fhed for drying have been lately erected on fome ground at the back of this prifon. The convicts here are allowed three-pence a day. The act for preferving the health of prifoners not hung up.

A *Table* of *Fees* to be taken at the Houfe of Correction at *Clerkenwell.*

	£.	s.	d.
For keeping and difcharging every prifoner committed by warrant, and turning the key at every fuch prifoner's difcharge	0	7	0
For a copy of every commitment	0	1	4
For going with any prifoner before a juftice	0	1	0
Prifoners brought in by conftables of the night and carried before a juftice	0	4	0

WHITECHAPEL PRISON, for DEBTORS.

THIS is a prifon for the liberty and manor of Stepney, and Hackney. The former includes, by a printed lift which I have, towns, parifhes, villages, ftreets, lanes, &c. to the number of forty-fix; and was granted by king Edward VI. to lord Wentworth, and his heirs for ever.

* This is a falutary employment, as the ftrong fcent of the pitch and tar may counteract any contagious or unhealthy effluvia in the work-rooms.

In

In it are confined thofe whofe debts are above £2, and under £5. The mafter's-fide prifoners have four fizeable chambers, fronting the road; i. e. two on each ftory. They pay 2s. 6d. a week; and lie two in a bed; two beds in a room. The common-fide debtors are in two long rooms in the court, near the tap-room; men in one room, women in the other: the court-yard in common. They hang out a begging-box from a little clofet in the front of the houfe; and attend it in turn. It brings them only a few pence a day; and of this pittance none partake but thofe who at entrance have paid the keeper 2s. 6d. and treated the prifoners with half a gallon of beer. When I was there in 1777, no more than three had purchafed this privilege.

The prifon is out of repair. It is the property of the lady of the manor. The keeper, *George Garred*, is an officer: he pays rent £24; and window-tax, and all other taxes. He keeps the tap. Fees, £0 : 8 : 1. No table: But in November 1776, I faw a paper hung up, on which was written as follows;

A *Table* of *Fees* to be taken by the Keeper of this Prifon.

	L.	s.	d.
For the difcharge of every perfon upon any civil action, procefs or execution	0	8	1
For every perfon who choofes to lay on the mafter-fide, for the firft night	0	2	0
For every perfon who choofes to lie on the mafter-fide after the firft night to pay every week	0	2	6

TOWER HAMLETS GAOL, in WELL-CLOSE SQUARE.

THIS prifon is at a public houfe, kept by an honeft Swede, who is gaoler. There is a court-room in the houfe for the Tower Hamlets. The prifon-yard is 116 feet by 18, latticed over the head. At one end, are two large rooms;

rooms; of which little ufe has been made fince the laft war, when French prifoners were kept in them. The prefent prifon-rooms are towards the other end of the court: On the ground floor is a day-room or clofet about $5\frac{1}{2}$ feet by $3\frac{1}{2}$, with a chimney. Up ftairs are three night rooms. Debtors from the court of requefts are fent to Clerkenwell bridewell. The prifon is quite out of repair, and not fecure. Keeper no falary: Fees, 9s. 1d. No table. Allowance, from a penny to two-pence a day. No ftraw.

St CATHARiNE's PRISON, for DEBTORS.

THIS prifon, rebuilt about ten years ago, is a fmall houfe of two ftories; two rooms on a floor. In April, 1774, there was a keeper, but no prifoners. I have fince that called two or three times, and found the houfe uninhabited: In Auguft, 1779, it was inhabited, but there were no prifoners.

THE SAVOY.

THIS prifon for foldiers, has two rooms called the *Guard Rooms*; becaufe in them are confined offenders who are of the king's guards. The remainder of the building near the gate is the keeper's houfe. On the oppofite fide of the court, is a large room down five fteps, the *Hall*: The rooms over it ufelefs. On the left-hand fide of the court is another hall, not fo large: At each end of it is a room with barrack bedfteads and beds; both rooms very clofe and unhealthy. Over them are other barrack-rooms, fomewhat more airy: One of them, No. 4. is tolerable, and has oppofite windows. There are, befides, the *Black Hole*, the *Condemn'd Hole*, the *Cock Pit*, and feveral other parts of this irregular building, which I pafs over.

TOTHILL.

TOTHILL-FIELDS BRIDEWELL.

KEEPER,   *George Smith.*
Salary,   £.50, paying the widow of the former keeper £20.
Fees,   £0 : 5 : 2.
Tranſports, taken by Mr Akermen.
.   Licence, Beer and Wine.

PRISONERS,
Allowance, a penny loaf, and a penny a day each.
Garniſh,   £0 : 1 : 4.

Number,	Priſoners.		Priſoners.
1774, April 22,	38.	1778, Jan. 8,	110.
1775, March 4,	109.	1779, Aug. 5,	74.
1776, March 6,	86.	Impreſſed Men	10.
—— May 3,	75.		

CHAPLAIN, None.

SURGEON, Mr *Glover.*
Salary,   £20.

This priſon has—For men, two day-rooms and three night-rooms—For faulty apprentices, five rooms, ten feet by ſeven—For women, a day-room, and four night-rooms. All the night-rooms have barrack beds. They are conſtantly waſhed every day; and are quite wholeſome. The priſoners waſh their hands and faces every morning before they come for their allowance. No ſtraw, No infirmary. A little room uſed as a ſurgery. A chapel, in which Mr Smith reads a chapter, and prayers every morning.

The women ſhould have another day-room: and one of the day-rooms, for men ſhould be enlarged. There would then be leſs quarrelling among them: and priſoners who are now idle might be employed. The courts adjacent might alſo be enlarged. The rooms for women, and their court, are *now* more airy, the garden-pales being ſet farther off. The keeper pays window-tax, and for water. Over the gate is a paper with this inſcription:

" N.

" No perfon admitted into this prifon on a Sunday after nine o'clock in the morning until five in the evening."

A TABLE of FEES

Allowed by the Governor of *Tothill-fields Bridewell*, as by order of Court January Seffions 1772.

	£.	s.	d.
For commitment and difcharge of a prifoner by warrant —	0	4	2
For the turnkey — — — —	0	1	0
Copy of commitment — — —	0	1	4
For a night's charge — — —	0	1	0

WESTMINSTER GATE-HOUSE.

THIS prifon, the property of the Dean and Chapter, was over two gate ways: but being in a very ruinous condition. has been taken down : and another is erected in Tothill-fields, joining to the bridewell, but not yet in-habited, Aug. 5, 1779. There will be a proper fepa-ration of debtors and felons ; and in the court of the lat-ter are four fmall rooms for the refractory. Both debtors and felons, though not feen by one another, will be to view from the pulpit, and there the keeper can eafily ob-ferve them when they are locked up. The courts will be plentifully fupplied with water, by pipes from the *main*. The outer wails are too low, fo that tools, &c. may be conveyed over.

THE KING's BENCH PRISON,

FOR DEBTORS.

MARSHALL,   *Thomas Thomas*, Efq.

DEPUTY MARSHAL,   *Thomas Marfin*, Efq now Mr *Farmer Shillingford*.

Salary
Fees,   *See Table*.
Licence, Beer and Wine. Tap let.

PRISONERS,

PRISONERS,
  Allowance, none.
  Garnith,   £0 : 2 : 0.
  Number,   —   In the Houfe.   In the Rules
    1774,   April 26,   324,   —   100.
    1776,   Jan. 28,   364,   —   80.
    1779,   Aug. 11,   511,   —   —   75.
    ——   Oct. 26,   438,   —   —   60.

CHAPLAIN, Rev. Mr *Evans*.
  Duty,   Sunday once : The facrament once month.
  Salary,   £0 : 2 : 0. on every commitment.

SURGEON, None.

This prifon is part old buildings, part new.

The old buildings are—a coffee-room juft within the gate—and a ftreet called *King-ftreet*. On the right hand is the tap-houfe; and four houfes for prifoners: each confifting of a ground floor, and two floors of chambers; four rooms on each floor; near 10 feet fquare, and 7 high. On the left-hand fide of the ftreet is the chapel; and fix houfes for prifoners; of equal depth with the former houfes: but the back-rooms have not, as the former have, communication with the fore-rooms. At the hither end of the fore-rooms, on the ground floor, is a common kitchen much too fmall. The cook, a prifoner, has the room over it. Thefe houfes alfo have ground-rooms, and two floors of chambers. All the rooms fronting King-ftreet, and the whole of the houfes on the other fide of the way, are for mafter's-fide debtors; who pay for each room unfurnifhed a fhilling a week. The back-part of the left-hand row is the common-fide; the doors in the back-front. The firft room on the ground floor they call their court-room. The two houfes at the farther end have fix rooms each, for crown-debtors and fines; and are called Crown-court. The reft of this range on all the three floors is for common-fide debtors. At the farther end of

L   King-

King-ſtreet, in a ſmall court encloſed from the reſt of the
yard, is a building called the *State-houſe ;* conſiſting of
ground floors, and two floors of chambers ; four ſizeable
rooms on each floor ; total twelve. A debtor who chooſes
to be here, pays the marſhal from eight to ten guineas
for his whole time ; beſides a ſhilling a week, like other
maſter's-ſide debtors.

M A R S H A L S E A   P R I S O N.

DEPUTY MARSHAL, *Thomas Marſon,* Eſq; now deceaſed.
Subſtitute, *Thomas Phillips,* now *William Williams.*
Salary,
Fees,   £0 : 10 : 10.
Licence,   Beer and Wine. The Tap let.

PRISONERS,
Allowance, none.
Garniſh,   £0 : 5 : 4. It is called ward-dues for coals &c.

CHAPLAIN, Rev. Mr *Cockane.*
Duty,   Sunday,
Salary,   1*s.* from each priſoner on diſcharge. *See Tab. Fees.*

SURGEONS, Meſſrs *Stapleton* and *Walſhman.*
Salary,   1*s.* from each priſoner on diſcharge. *See Tab. Fees.*

To this priſon of the Court of Marſhalſea, and of the
King's Palace-Court of Weſtminſter, are brought debtors
arreſted for the loweſt ſums, any where within twelve
miles of the palace, except in the city of London : and alſo
perſons committed for piracy.

The deputy marſhal, under whoſe particular cuſtody
this priſon is, has his appointment from the knight marſhal of the king's houſehold for the time being. The
great abuſes practiſed by this officer were reported to parliament by the gaol Committeee in 1729.

The priſon is too ſmall, and greatly out of repair. Little
regard is ſhewn to the laſt act for white-waſhing and cleaning

ing the rooms. No infirmary. The court is well fupplied with water. In it the prifoners play at racke's, miffifippi &c. and in a little back court, the *Park*, at fkittles.

A TABLE OF FEES.

To be taken by the Gaoler or Keeper of the Maifhalfea Prifon—on any Civil Action—fettled—the 17th Day of May 1765 Purfuant to an Act for Relief of Debtors &c.

	£.	s.	d.
To the knight marfhal upon the difcharge of every prifoner charged with one or more actions	0	1	8
To the keeper for his care and fafe cuftody of every prifoner upon the difcharge of fuch prifoner on the firft action	0	4	8
To the keeper upon the difcharge of fuch prifoner charged with one or more actions after the firft	0	3	8
To the furgeon or apothecary on the difcharge of every prifoner charged with one or more actions	0	1	0
To the chaplain on the like difcharge	0	1	0
To the turnkey upon the difcharge of every prifoner on the firft action	0	1	6
To the turnkey upon the difcharge of fuch prifoner charged with one or more actions after the firft	0	1	0
To the clerk for entering the difcharge of a prifoner on one or more actions	0	1	0
To the keeper for the ufe of bed, bedding and fheets for every prifoner if found by the gaoler at the prifoner's requeft, for the firft night on the mafter's fide of the faid prifon.	0	0	6
And every night after the firft night	0	0	3
And if two lie in a bed 2d. each	0	0	4

No other fee for the ufe of chamber, bed, bedding, or upon the difcharge or commitment of any prifoner on any civil action.

BOROUGH COMPTER.

GAOLER, *Jeremiah Beavis.*
Salary, none.
Fees,   Debtors, £0 : 7 : 0.
         Felons,   0 : 11 : 4.
Tranfports,   0 : 10 : 6. from the contractor.
Licence, Beer and Wine.

PRISONERS,

Allowance, Debtors, } a penny loaf a day each *(weight in Aug.*
           Felons,   }   1779, 12 oz.)
Garnifh, £0 : 2 : 8. mafter's-fide.
          0 : 1 : 4 common-fide.

CHAP.

CHAPLAIN, None.
SURGEON, None.

This prifon, in Tooley-ftreet, for the borough of South-wark, which contains four parifhes and a part of a fifth, has, for mafter's-fide debtors, feven rooms—for common-fide debtors, a room on the ground floor, in which felons &c. are with them night and day: a long room up ftairs, the *Rookery*, and a room over it, ufelefs, becaufe not fe-cure.—The women are in the ftone kitchen, now divided into two rooms. Three of the common-fide rooms have barrack beds. Among the debtors are many poor creatures from the court of confcience, who lie there till their debts are paid.—There is a fmall court; and a chapel, but no chaplain is appointed.

The whole prifon is much out of repair, and ruinous. No infirmary. No bedding or ftraw. The keeper, an of-ficer, pays window-tax and land-tax. He is put in by the high bailiff, whofe office is in the difpofal of the court of aldermen.—An infcription over the gate, dated 1716, calls it the *Borough Court:* but the courts are now held at St Margaret's Hill.

F   E   E   S.

	£.	s.	d.
For the admiffion of every prifoner for felony trefpafs affault or other mifdemeanours — — —	0	11	4
For every night's lodging — — —	0	0	6
To the turnkey for the difmiffion of every fuch prifoner	0	1	0
For every prifoner brought by a peace officer for fafe cuftody until hearing can be had before a magiftrate — —	0	2	0

COUNTY GAOL at HERTFORD.

GAOLER, *Cornelius Wilfon.*
 Salary, none. £39 : 6 : 10. to fupply the felons with bread,
            as below.
 Fees, Debtors, } 0 : 15 : 4.
   Felons,

Tran-

. Tranfports, £1 : 1 : o each to London.
Licence, Beer and Wine.

PRISONERS.
Allowance, Debtors, none.
Felons, 1*lb.* of bread a day farmed by the gaoler.
Garnifh, £0 : 4 : 6.

CHAPLAIN, Rev. Mr *Scott,* now Rev. Mr *Moore.*
Duty, Sunday ; and one other day not fixed.
Salary, £40.

SURGEON, Mr *Cu!ler.*
Salary, £10.

This gaol, built in 1702, is in the middle of the town. In front are two fmall day-rooms, for felons, in which they are always locked up: no fire-place.—Their dungeons or night-rooms are, one down 18 fteps, the other 19. Over their day-rooms, is a large lumber-room ; and joining to it a lodging-room for women-felons. On each fide of it are two rooms on the ground floor, and two chambers for debtors. No chapel. No infirmary. The act for pre-ferving the health of prifoners not hung up.

In the interval of two of my vifits the gaol fever prevail-ed, and carried off feven or eight prifoners, and two turn-keys. *

A TABLE OF FEES.

£. s. d.

For the chamber-rent, bed and bedding of each debtor *per-night* pro-vided that no more than two be put into one bed nor more than two beds in one room — — — 0 0 4
For the chamber-rent, bed and bedding of each prifoner upon cri-minal procefs *per week* provided that no more than two be put in-to one bed ; nor more than two beds in the fame room 0 3 6

---

* I was well informed, that a prifoner brought out as dead, from one of the dungeons, on being *wafhed under the pump,* fhewed figns of life, and foon after recovered. Since this, I have known *other* inftances of the fame kind.

For

	£.	s.	d.
For the turnkey's fees into gaol　—　—	0	1	0
For the turnkey's fees out of gaol　—　—	0	1	0
For the gaoler's fees upon each prisoner discharged　—	0	13	4

E S S E X.

COUNTY GAOL AT CHELMSFORD.

G A O L E R, *Sufanna Taylor.*
　　Salary,　　none.

　　Fees,　　Debtors, } £0 : 15 : 4.
　　　　　　Felons,

　Tranfports, to London or Gravefend, £1 : 5 : 0. for each, if not more than feven, for each above feven £1 : 1 : 0.
　　Licence,　　Beer and Wine.

PRISONERS,

　　Allowance,　Debtors, } a pound and half of bread a day, and
　　　　　　　Felons, 　　　　　a quart of fmall beer.

　　Garnifh,　　Debtors, £0 : 4 : 6.
　　　　　　　Felons,　0 : 5 : 0.

C H A P L A I N, *now* Rev. Mr *Morgan.*
　　Duty,　　Sunday.
　　Salary,　　£40, now 50.

S U R G E O N, Mr *Griffinhooft.*
　　Salary,　　£25, for felons, and the bridewell prifoners.

A *clofe* prifon, frequently infected with the gaol-diftemper. Inquiring in October 1775, for the head-turnkey, I was told he died of it.

In the tap-room there hung a paper on which, among other things, was written, " Prifoners to pay garnifh or run the gantlet."

Debtors have a bufhel of coals a day from about 12th November to Lady Day and £5 : 0 : 0 a year by a legacy of Elizabeth Herris from lands in Brentwood, paid by the rector or minifter of the parifh of Clemsford on the 25th of December. By a memorial hung up in the
tap-

tap-room, it appears the bequeſt was acknowledged by the teſtatrix 14th June 1476.—It was generous in the juſtices to grant debtors the ſame allowance as felons; and very judicious to fix that allowance to a *certain weight.*

There is a new gaol, which exceeds the old one in ſtrength &c. almoſt as much as in ſplendour. This county, to their honour, have ſpared no coſt.

A TABLE OF FEES.

	£.	s.	d.
For the chamber-rent bed and bedding of each debtor provided that no more than two be put into one bed, nor more than two beds in the ſame room — — — —	0	0	4
For the chamber-rent bed and bedding of each priſoner upon crimi-nal procefs *per week* provided that no more than two be put into one bed nor more than two beds in one room —	0	3	6
For the turnkey's fee into gaol — — —	0	1	0
For the turnkey's fee out of gaol — —	0	1	0
For the gaoler's fee upon each priſoner's difcharge —	0	13	4

COUNTY GAOL at MAIDSTONE.

GAOLER, *Philip De'tillin.*
    Salary,   £60, inſtead of the tap.
    Fees,   Debtors, £0 : 12 : 4.
             Felons,   0 : 15 : 4.
    Tranſports,   0 : 15 : 0. each, and the fees.
    Licence, none. *See Salary.*

PRISONERS,
    Allowance, Debtors, none.
             Felons, a loaf once in two days *(weight 2lb. 4oz. Feb.* 1776) and every day a quart of ſmall beer.
    Garniſh,   Debtors, 0 : 3 : 0.
             Felons, 0 : 1 : 6.
CHAPLAIN, Rev. Mr *Hudfon.*
    Duty,   Sunday and Wednefday.
    Salary,   £30; lately augmented to 50l.
SURGEON, Mr *Waller.*
    Salary,   £50, for the gaol and bridewell.

This

This gaol was erected in 1746, as appears by the date. The rooms in the felons' ward are fizeable ; but the air is obftructed by wooden bars at the windows (three inches and a half broad) inftead of iron ones.   There are three courts : one for debtors ; one for men-felons ; and one for women-felons.   The two laft are much too fmall ; but may be commodioufly enlarged, by adding to them the adjacent court of the old bridewell.

Felons are allowed yearly ten chaldron of coals : they have barrack beds*, and hop bagging with ftraw ; but no coverlets.   This county has for years paft been fo confiderate as to pay the fees of poor prifoners acquitted : and to tranfports caft at affizes, who are entitled to the king's allowance of 2s. 6d. a week, they continue the allowance which they had before trial.   They alfo pay the gaoler's fees for thofe convicts.

A T A B L E O F F E E S.

	£.	s.	d.
For the difcharge from the faid gaol of every prifoner committed for treafon, felony or any offence againft his majefty's peace to the gaoler or keeper — —	0	13	4
To turnkey on commitment of every fuch prifoner —	0	1	0
To him more on the difcharge of every fuch prifoner	0	1	0
On the commitment or coming into gaol of every prifoner in a civil action, to the faid gaoler or keeper —	0	3	0
On the difcharge of every fuch prifoner to the faid gaoler or keeper — — — —	†0	7	10
And to the turnkey — —	0	1	6
For the ufe of bed bedding and fheets for each of the faid laft-mentioned prifoners on the mafter's fide of the faid prifon for the firft night to the faid gaoler or keeper —	0	0	6
And for every night after the firft — —	0	0	3
And if two fuch perfons lie together in one bed then	0	0	2

* Barrack beds are low ftages of boards, raifed from the floor, and floping from the wall towards the middle of the room ; as in the barracks for foldiers.

† Thofe figures 0 7 10 are written upon a rafure.

For

£. s. d.

For every fuch prifoner as fhall chufe to be on the mafter's-
 fide for the ufe of the bed, bedding and fheets the firft night 0 0 6
For every night after the firft — — 0 0 3
But if two fuch prifoners lie together then two-pence each 0 0 4
If any fuch prifoner through poverty can only provide a couch,
 then to the faid gaoler or keeper for chamber-rent *per*
 week — — — — 0 0 1

CANTERBURY CITY GAOL,

Over the Weft-gate. One large day-room for men and
women : And in each of the two towers, a fmall night-
room. No court ; and prifoners are feldom permitted to
walk on the leads. Allowance, three pennyworth of bread
a day. Keeper's falary, £5. Fees, debtors, 6s. 8d. felons 13s. 4d. No table. He keeps a public houfe adjoining, in which is a room or two for mafter's-fide debtors.
No regard is paid to the claufe enjoining that " once in
the year at leaft" the gaols fhall be white-wafhed.

ROCHESTER CITY GAOL,

Under the court-room. One day-room to the ftreet ;
and two inner or night-rooms : All clofe and offenfive.
In the keeper's houfe is a room for fuch debtors as can
pay for a bed : And another in which women-felons were
kept when the affizes were held here. No court : No
water acceffible to prifoners. Allowance, two pence a
day. Keeper, a ferjeant : No falary : Fees 6s. No table.
At my vifit in 1779, I found two debtors who had been
locked up fome weeks in the clofe offenfive room next the
ftreet.—The court-room was built, as appears by the date,
in 1687, and it is probable, there has been no alteration
in the prifon fince that time.

M   DOVER

D O V E R   C A S T L E,

For Debtors in the Cinque-Ports, i. e. *Haflings, Dover, Hyth, Romney,* and *Sandwich.*

The Earl of *Holdernefs* was conftable; now *Frederick* Lord *North* is conftable, and *Henry Wood* bodar. Two rooms: No court: No water. Entrance fee, £1 : 6 : 8. Keeper is bailiff for the Cinque-Ports; falary, £30. His prifon dirty: His apology for it was, that " he had been abfent fome weeks on his bufinefs as an officer." At my laft vifit the rooms were white-wafhed, and much cleaner than at my former vifit.

D O V E R   T O W N   G A O L.

One room of it is the bridewell. The gaol is two rooms on the ground floor, and two above. No fire-places. All clofe and offenfive; but at my laft vifit it was much cleaner, and no company were drinking there, as the new keeper has *no* licence. The court not fecure. Allowance, four pence a day. Keeper's falary, £10. and a chaldron of coals: Fees, 8s. 2d. No table.

S U S S E X.

C O U N T Y   G A O L   at   H O R S H A M:

G A O L E R,	*Charles Cooper.*	
Salary,	£120 of late: in lieu of all fees.	
Fees,	Debtors, Felons,	} £1 : 4 : 10.
Tranfports,		2 : 2 : 0. each.
Licence,	Wine.	

P R I S O N E R S,
Allowance, Debtors, none.
Felons, two pennyworth of bread a day: *now* 2lb.
Garnifh, £0 : 6 : 6.

CHAPLAIN,

CHAPLAIN, None. But the clergyman who attends condemned criminals has £5. a year.

SURGEON, lately dead.
  Salary,   £5. for felons.

The rooms are too fmall, except the free-ward for debtors. No ftraw : No court ; and yet ground enough for one behind the gaol. Tranfports convicted at quarter feffions, have as thofe condemned at affize, the king's allowance of 2s. 6d. a week. Lent affize at Eaft-Grinftead ; where there is no prifon : Summer affize, at Lewes and Horfham alternately.

The new gaol that was building in 1776, is now finifhed.

A TABLE of FEES.

			£.	s.	d.
Upon the difcharge of every debtor	—	—	1	2	4
The fheriff's fee thereupon	—	—	0	11	8
Turnkey thereupon	—	—	0	2	6
For every peck of charcoal	—	—	0	0	3
For every fagot	—	—	0	0	2½
For every quart of fmall beer	—	—	0	0	0½
For lodgings in the gaoler's beds by the week	—	0	2	0
Upon the difcharge of every felon, to the gaoler	—	1	2	4

COUNTY GAOL in SOUTHWARK.

GAOLER,   Benjamin Hall.
  Salary,   none.
  Fees,   Debtors, £0 : 12 : 4.
             Felons,   0 : 15 : 4.
  Licence,   Beer and Wine. The Tap let.

PRISONERS,
       ance, Debtors, } three halfpennyworth of bread a day
             Felons, } (weight 17 ounces, Dec. 1776, and Aug.
                        1779).
  Garnifh, Debtors, £0 : 4 : 6.
            Felons,   0 : 1 : 0.
                              M 2   CHAPLAIN,

CHAPLAIN, Rev. Mr *Dyer*.
    Duty,   Sunday.
    Salary,   £50.

SURGEON, Meſſrs *Burt* and Co.
    Salary,   £20. for this gaol, and the bridewell in St George's
        Fields ; and £5. for travelling charges to report at the
        quarter ſeſſions, the ſtate of the priſoners.

The New Gaol, beſides the gaoler's houſe, and the tap-room, has—for maſter's-ſide debtors, a parlour, and four other ſizeable rooms ; and for common-ſide debtors, three good rooms. Mr Hall prevents their being crowded with the wives and children of the debtors. For theſe priſoners, there is a court ; into which felons are not ad-mitted ; except a few, whom the gaoler has reaſons for indulging with that diſtinction.

The ward for men-felons has ſix rooms on three floors : In theſe they ſleep. There is a court belonging to it.— The ward for women-felons has two lower rooms, two above ; and a court belonging to it. In the two upper rooms, are put malefactors of either ſex condemned to die. I have here noted 18 rooms : Yet they are not ſuf-ficient for the number of priſoners. Mr Hall is ſometimes obliged to put men-felons into ſome rooms of the women's ward. In ſo cloſe a priſon ſituated in a populous neigh-bourhood, I did not wonder to ſee in March 1776 ſeveral felons ſick on the floors. No bedding nor ſtraw : No infirmary : No chapel : Divine ſervice is performed in the parlour ; which is too ſmall for the purpoſe ; about 16 feet ſquare. The act for preſerving the health of priſoners is on a painted board. The clauſes againſt ſpirituous li-quors are hung up.

A

A TABLE of FEES.

	£.	s.	d.
For the difcharge from the faid gaol of every prifoner committed for treafon, or felony or any offence againft his majefty's peace, to the gaoler or keeper	0	13	4
To the turnkey on every committment of fuch prifoner	0	1	0
To the turnkey on the difcharge of every fuch prifoner	0	1	0
On the commitment or coming into gaol of every prifoner in a civil action, to the faid gaoler or keeper	0	3	0
On the difcharge of every fuch prifoner, to the faid gaoler or keeper	0	6	10
And to the turnkey	0	1	6
For the ufe of bed bedding and fheets for each of the faid mentioned prifoners on the mafter's fide of the faid prifon, for the firft night, to the faid gaoler or keeper	0	0	6
And for every night after the firft	0	0	2
But if two fuch perfons lie together in one bed, then one penny half-penny each	0	0	3
To the clerk of the papers on every difcharge of any prifoner in a civil action	0	1	0
For every fuch prifoner as fhall chufe to be on the mafter-fide, for the ufe of bed and bedding and fheets the firft night	0	0	6
For every night after the firft	0	0	3
But if two fuch prifoners lie together in one bed, then two pence each	0	0	4
If any fuch prifoner through poverty can only provide a couch, then to the faid gaoler or keeper for chamber-rent *per week*	0	0	1

COUNTY GAOL at AYLESBURY.

GAOLER, Thomas Smith.
 Salary, none.
 Fees, Debtors, £0 : 15 : 10.
   Felons, 0 : 18 : 4.
 Licence, Beer and Wine.

PRISONERS,
 Garnifh, Debtors, £0 : 8 : 0.
   Felons, 0 : 2 : 6.

CHAPLAIN, Rev. Mr Hopkins.
 Duty, Sunday.
 Salary, £40.

SURGEON, Mr Ludgate.
 Salary, £20. for debtors, felons, and the bridewell.

One court. A hall for *debtors*; and fundry rooms for the mafter's-fide: But no free ward. In the felons' day-room

room is an oven for purifying the cloths. A fmall night-room for women-felons. Two condemned rooms. In the interval of my firft and fecond vifit, fix or feven died of the gaol diftemper. At my vifits in 1776, after the appointing Mr Ludgate, all the prifoners were well. At my laft vifit, two men fentenced for three years had continued here two years and a half; one of them was much emaciated by confinement without work. * No infirmary. Divine fervice is performed in the fhire-hall, which joins to the prifon. No table of fees. Claufes againft fpirituous liquors, and act for preferving the health of prifoners not hung up. Mr Smith contracts to fupply debtors and felons with a pound of bread a day, and two hot dinners a week; and to convey tranfports to London; for £70. a year. At fummer affize, prifoners are moved from hence to Buckingham.

COUNTY GAOL AT HUNTINGDON.

GAOLER. *Henry Blanc*, afterwards *Robert Nunn*, now *John Randall*.

Salary, none.

Fees, Debtors, £0 : 12 : 6.
Felons, 0 : 15 : 10.

Tranfports, If only one, £12; if more, £9 each: He paying the clerk of affize a guinea for each.

Licence, Beer.

PRISONERS,

Allowance, Debtors, none.
Felons, four halfquartern-loaves a week.

Garnifh, Debtors, £0 : 2 : 6.

CHAPLAIN, Rev. Mr *Brock*. Now no Chaplain.

SURGEON, Mr *Hunt*, now Mr *Perkins*.

Salary, £5 : 5 : 0.

---

* The furgeon and gaoler both informed me, that three men brought from Hertford gaol the Lent affize 1778, had their toes mortified; which being fimilar to what I once faw in that gaol, I could the more eafily credit it.

Thia

This gaol is alfo the *County Bridewell* and *Town Gaol.*

For debtors, a day-room or kitchen ; and over it a large lodging room. Near it is a day-room for felons : and down 9 fteps a dungeon for men-felons ; in which is a fmall condemned room. In another place, down 7 fteps, is a dungeon for women-felons : The floor of it level with the court ; in which is the bridewell. This has two rooms below for men ; and two above for women. The prifon and court are too fmall : But I always found the whole remarkably clean, except at my laft vifit. Claufes againft fpiritous liquors hung up. The act for preferving the health of prifoners not hung up. No infirmary. Salary for the bridewell, £24 : 16 : 0 : For the town gaol, £3. —Straw, £4 : 16 : 0. a year.

I was forry to hear at my vifit in 1776, that Mr Brock, the late chaplain, who officiated very conftantly twice a week, and had a falary of £20. was difmiffed. He would have continued his attendance without the falary ; but an order was made exprefsly forbidding it.

COUNTY GAOL, CAMBRIDGE CASTLE.

GAOLER, *Simeon Saunders.*
  Salary, £12 : 14 : 0.
  Fees,   Debtors, £0 : 14 : 8.
      Felons, 0 ; 10 : 8.
  Tranfports, £6 : 6 : 0 each : he paying the clerk of affize
      £1 : 1 : 0 for each.
  Licence, Beer.

PRISONERS,
  Allowance, Debtors, none.
      Felons, two pence a day.
  Garnifh, Debtors, £0 : 5 : 4.
      Felons, 0 : 1 : 3.

CHAPLAIN,

CHAPLAIN, None.

SURGEON, Mr *Prince*.
    Salary, none ; he makes a bill.

The prifon is the gate of the old Caftle. Below are two ftrong rooms ; one for men-felons ; the other for women. You go up 22 ftone fteps on the outfide to the debtors' apartments. On the firft floor is a room for the turnkey ; a large kitchen ; and two or three other rooms. Above them are five rooms and a condemned room. All the rooms are fizeable.—Claufes of act againft fpirituous liquors hung up, by a written order of Thomas Cockran, Efq; fheriff.—The act for preferving the health of prifoners not hung up. Straw, twenty fhillings a year. The caftle yard is fpacious, but not fafe ; and prifoners have not the ufe of it. In it is the gallows.

Debtors have fome relief from legacies and donations paid by feveral colleges : and twenty fhillings a year, deducting land-tax, from an eftate at Croxton in this county. No memorial in the prifon.

E L Y   G A O L.

GAOLER,   *John Allday*.
    Salary,   none.
    Fees,   Debtors,   £0 - 15 - 3.
            Felons,   0 - 13 - 4.
    Tranfports, £5. each
    Licence,   Beer.

PRISONERS,
    Allowance, Debtors, } none.
            Felons, }
        Garnifh,   £0 - 1 - 4.
CHAPLAIN,   None.
SURGEON,   None.

This

This gaol, the property of the bifhop, who is lord of the franchife of the ifle of Ely, was in part rebuilt by the late bifhop about fourteen years ago ; upon complaint of the cruel method * which, for want of a fafe gaol, the keeper took to fecure his prifoners.

COUNTY GAOL, NORWICH CASTLE.

GAOLER, George Gynne.
 Salary, none : He pays the under-fheriff £31 - 10 - 0
  per annum.
 Fees, Debtors, £0 - 7 - 8.
   Felons,   0 - 13 - 4.
 Tranfports,   5 - 15 - 6 each.
 Licence, Beer and Wine.

PRISONERS,

      a two-penny loaf each *per* day *(weight*
 Allowance, Debtors, *in Dec.* 1774, 10 *ounces)* and every
    Felons, week in common a ftone of cheefe ; in
      winter twelve bufhels of coals, in fum-
      mer fix bufhels.

 Garnifh, Debtors, £0 - 5 - 0.
   Felons,   0 - 1 - 0.

CHAPLAIN, Rev. Mr *Willins.*
 Duty, Friday.
 Salary, £30.

SURGEON, Mr *Palgrave,* now Mr *Brown.*
 Salary, now £40.

The caftle is fituated on the fummit of a hill. That part which is called the *upper gaol,* has ten rooms for mafter's-
      N   .fide

---

* This was by chaining them down on their backs upon a floor, acrofs which were feveral iron bars ; with an iron collar with fpikes about their necks, and a heavy iron bar over their legs. An excellent magiftrate, James Collyer, Efq; prefented an account of the cafe, accompanied with a draw-ing, to the king; with which his majefty was much affected, and gave im-mediate orders for a proper inquiry and redrefs.

fide debtors; and leads for them to walk on. The *low gaol* has feveral rooms for debtors, felons, &c. A fmall area in the middle of the gaol, in which are lately made fome improvements; fuch as a pump, a convenient bath, and fome rooms over it. There is a dungeon down a ladder of 8 fteps, for men-felons; in which has often been an inch or two of water: And only a fmall room for women felons; fo that they cannot be feparate from the men, when decency would moft of all require it. At my vifit in 1779, there were barrack beds in the dungeon. There are too airy rooms for the fick; fo diftinct from the reft of the prifon, that there is no danger of fpreading any infection from thence. The gaoler is humane, and refpected by his prifoners. Thefe, felons as well as debtors, fell at the grates of their feparate day-rooms, laces, garters, purfes, nets &c. of their own making.

NORWICH CITY AND COUNTY GAOL.

GAOLER,	*Benjamin Fakenham.*	
Salary,	none · He pays the under-fheriff £40 a year.	
Fees,	Debtors, £0 - 6 - 8.	
	Felons, 0 - 13 - 4.	
Tranfports,	5 - 5 - 0 each.	
Licenee,	Beer and Wine.	
PRISONERS,		
Allowance,	Debtors, ⎫	a two-penny loaf each : In 1776, it
	Felons, ⎬	was reduced to a penny loaf; in
	⎭	1779, 12 *oz.* of bread.
Garnifh,	£0 - 1 - 0.	
CHAPLAIN,	Rev. Mr *Buckle,*	
Duty,	Prayers, once a fortnight; fermon one Tuefday in a month.	
Salary,	£20.	
SURGEON,	Mr *Matchett.*	
Salary,	£5 - 5 - 0 for debtors and felons.	

Only.

Only one court. Many rooms for mafter's-fide debtors. One room for common-fide debtors, who are freemen. There is no room for thofe who are not free, but the felons' day-room; which is under the other, and down 13 fteps. The felons' dungeons, or night-rooms, are down 11 fteps; one of them quite dark; the other almoft fo. The women's dungeon down 10 fteps, has a fire-place: But at my late vifits they had another night room, about $10\frac{1}{4}$ feet by $5\frac{1}{2}$, and but 5 feet high. Straw was only £1 - 1 - 0 a year, but now £1 - 6 - 0.—The keeper's ftable adjoining to the laft room, would make the women a good feparate day-room.—Claufes againft fpirituous liquors hung up. Act for preferving the health of prifoners not hung up.

Many alterations are lately made for the better. The court is now paved: And fome old fheds, that were in it, are taken down. Three night rooms or cells for felons, about three feet below the ground, 8 feet fquare, planked all over. A bath: And over it two rooms for debtors. Over them two airy rooms for the fick; each 22 feet by 16, and near 12 feet high.

YARMOUTH TOWN GAOL.

Befides the gaoler's houfe, in which are rooms for mafter's-fide debtors, there are for all the prifoners, only a fmall day-room and court; and two or three lodging-rooms for fuch as pay for them: Two dungeons or night-rooms down a ladder of 10 fteps, one for men, the other for women. Allowance, a penny loaf a day (weight in Feb. 1776, 13 ounces): Four chaldron of coals a year. The corporation fends out a begging-bafket three times a week.—Gaoler's falary, £15. Fees, 6s. 8d. No table.

Claufes

Claufes againft fpirituous liquors, and the act for preferving the health of prifoners not hung up.

LYNN REGIS TOWN GAOL.

The rooms for debtors, felons, and petty offenders are convenient, and were clean at my firft vifit. Cribs with ftraw and two coverlets for the felons: The court is fmall, and has fowls kept in it. The act for preferving the health of prifoners not hung up. Gaoler's falary, £11; now £20: Fees, debtors 3s. 4d. felons 5s. per table figned by the mayor, dated 1729.

COUNTY GAOL at IPSWICH.

GAOLER, *Rowland Baker*, now *John Ripfhaw.*
  Salary, none.

Fees, Debtors, } £0 - 10 - 8.
      Felons, }

Tranfports, £6 - 6 - 0 each: He paying clerk of affize £1 - 1 - 0. for each.

  Licence, Beer and Wine.

PRISONERS,
  Allowance, Debtors, none.
    Felons, two pence a day in bread *(weight in Dec. 1774, 18 ounces and a half.)*

  Garnifh, Debtors, £0 - 2 - 6.
      Felons, 0 - 1 - 0.

CHAPLAIN, Rev. Mr *Brome.*
  Duty, Sunday and Friday.
  Salary, £50.

SURGEON,
  Salary, £40 for debtors and felons.

This is alfo the *town gaol*: Yet only one court-yard.— For debtors, a kitchen, or day-room; and feveral chambers: One of thefe is lately made a free ward.—For women felons a day-room: And for the men a ftrong night-room; with beds excellently contrived for cleanlinefs and health. Each prifoner has a crib-bedftead, 10 or 12 inches high; the

the head raifed a few inches; ftrong feet, low fides. Thefe keep as diftinct as poffible, prifoners who fleep in the fame room; and are eafily moved when the ward is to be wafhed. The county allows to each crib a ftraw bed, and a blanket.—The women have no feparate day-room: And their ward, or night-room, has no fire-place. One of the two drinking-rooms is called the *gar-nifh-room*.—Two rooms for the fick; not diftinct enough from the reft. It is not without reluctance that I add, the fick in February 1776 complained to me of being neglected by the furgeon. At my two laft vifits, none fick.— Debtors fell at the front grate, garters, purfes, &c. of their own making. In 1779, I found this prifon clean, though full of prifoners. The water from the pump is conveyed through the fewers, which prevents the court-yard, which is fmall, from being offenfive.

WARWICKSHIRE.

COUNTY GAOL at WARWICK.

GAOLER, *William Roe* Jun.
 Salary,   none.
 Fees,   Debtors, £0 - 14 - 6.
     Felons,   0 - 13 - 4.
 Tranfports, £8 - 0 - 0 each, he paying clerk of affize £1 - 1 - 0
  for each.
 Licence to turnkey for beer. Gaoler brews it.

PRISONERS.
 Allowance, Debtors, none.
     Felons, a loaf of 3*lb.* every other day.
 Garnifh,   £0 - 2 - 6.

CHAPLAIN, Rev. Mr *Muffan.*
 Duty,   Sunday and Friday.
 Salary,   £50.

SURGEON, Mr *Weale.*
 Salary,   £20 for gaol and bridewell.

One court for debtors, and men-felons. Women-felons have quite feparate court, day-room, and two night-
rooms. They ufed to be loaded with irons; now they
have none. Men-felons have a day-room: Their night-
room is in an octagonal dungeon about 21 feet diameter,
down 31 fteps; clofe, damp, and offenfive. Two cells,
in another dungeon for the condemned. Prifoners are
tried in the county clothing. I faw twelve fuits for men,
and fix for women.

COVENTRY CITY AND COUNTY GAOL.

GAOLER,   *Bafil Goode.*
   Salary,   £12, *now* taken off.

   Fees,   Debtors, } £0 - 15 - 4.
            Felons, }

   Tranfports,   £8 each.
   Licence,   Beer.

PRISONERS.
   Allowance,   Debtors, none.
           Felons, a pennyworth of bread a day.
   Garnifh,   £0 - 3 - 0.

CHAPLAIN,   None.

SURGEON,   Mr *Harper.*
   Salary,   none: He makes a bill.

This gaol, built about 1772, is in a clofe part of the
city. I was fhewn a fine fpot which fome gentlemen very
judicioufly preferred. It has eight lodging-rooms for
mafter's-fide debtors; and the common ward. Women
felons have only one room, and that without a fire-place.
The men have a day room. To their *dungeons* you go
down twelve fteps to a paffage only four feet wide: The
                                                four

four dungeons are about nine feet by fix: At the upper corner of each, a little window. All are very damp, dirty, and offenfive: We went down with torches. Only one court for all prifoners. No ftraw. No infirmary. Many rooms might be made for criminals in the adjoining old county-hall; in which cafe the horrid dungeons need not be ufed, and the fexes might be feparated. Neither claufes againft fpirituous liquors, nor the act for preferving the health of prifoners, are hung up. There is now a table of fees.

BIRMINGHAM TOWN GAOL.

The gaol for this large populous town is called *the Dungeon*. The court is only about 25 feet fquare. Keeper's houfe in front; and under it two cells down 7 fteps: The ftraw is on bedfteads. On one fide of the court two nightrooms for women, 8 feet by 5 feet 9 inches; and fome rooms over them: On the other fide is the gaoler's ftable, and one fmall day-room for men and women; no window: Above is a free ward for court of confcience debtors, who are cleared in forty days: This is a fizeable room, but has only one window 18 inches fquare. Over it is another room, or two.

In this fmall court, befides the litter from the ftable, there was a ftagnant puddle near the fink, for the gaoler's ducks. (Gaoler's poultry is a very common nuifance; but in fo fcanty a court it is intollerable). The whole prifon is very offenfive. At fome particular times here are great numbers confined. Once in the winter 1775 there were above 150, who by the care of the magiftrates had a fupply of proper food, broth, &c. Licence for beer. Fees 2s. No table. Neither claufes againft fpirituous liquors,

quors, nor act for preserving the health of prisoners are hung up.

COUNTY GAOL at LEICESTER.

GAOLER,   *Samuel Jordan*, now *William Jordan*.
   Salary,   none.

   Fees,   Debtors, } £0 - 15 - 4.
         Felons, }

   Transports, If only one, £8 : if more than one, £7 each.
   Licence,   none.

PRISONERS,

   Allowance, Debtors, } a four-penny loaf every other day *(weight*
          Felons, } *once 2lb. 8oz. once 3lb. 5oz.)*.

   Garnish,   Debtors, £0 - 4 - 0.
         Felons,   0 - 3 - 0.

CHAPLAIN, Rev. Mr *Pigot.*
   Duty,   Sunday.
   Salary,   £30.

SURGEON,   Mr *Mason.*
   Salary,   £15 for debtors and felons.

For master's-side debtors nine or ten rooms. Day-room common. The free ward, *the cellar*, is a dungeon, 29½ feet by 8 feet 8 inches, and 6½ feet high, down 7 steps, and damp ; two windows ; the largest about fifteen inches square. Felons' day and night-rooms are dungeons from 5 to 7 steps under ground. They sleep on thick mats on the floor ; which, if coverlets were added, would be better than straw. The whole close and offensive. Court small. No chapel. Two rooms lately built for an infirmary : But the gaol is not convenient or healthy. In 1774, three debtors and a felon died of the small-pox. Of that disease I was informed few ever recover in this gaol. The castle-hill is near the shire-hall, and is a fine spot for air and water.

LEICESTER

LEICESTER TOWN AND COUNTY GAOL.

GAOLER, *Henry Coulfon,* now *Samuel Jordan.*
 Salary, none : He pays rent £3.

 Fees, Debtors, } £0 - 15 - 4.
    Felons, }

 Tranfports, £10 each.
 Licence, Beer.

PRISONERS,
 Allowance, Debtors, } two pence a day each in bread.
    Felons, }

 Garnifh, Debtors, £0 - 4 - 6.
    Felons, 0 - 2 - 6.

CHAPLAIN, None.

SURGEON, Mr *Maule.*
 Salary, none : He makes a bill.

A common day-room or kitchen : Two rooms above for fuch as pay. Down five fteps a dungeon for men-felons; another for women; another for common-fide debtors. This town gaol has a court with plenty of water. Neither claufes againft fpirituous liquors, nor the act for preferving the health of prifoners, are hung up; but there is *now* a table of fees.

C O U N T Y G A O L AT D E R B Y.

GAOLER, *Blyth Simpfon.*
 Salary, £30.

 Fees, Debtors, } £0 - 17 - 4.
    Felons, }

 Tranfports, £5 - 17 - 0 each.
 Licence, Beer.

PRISONERS,

PRISONERS,

Allowance,	Debtors, Felons,	} *per* week, each two nine-penny loaves ; and in common two *Cwt* of coals.
Garnifh,	£0 - 3 - 6, and £0 - 1 - 2 for coals, &c.	

CHAPLAIN, Rev. Mr *Seal*, now the Rev. Mr *Henry*.
Duty,   Tuefday, Thurfday, Saturday.
Salary,   £30.

SURGEON,   Mr *Harrifon*.
Salary,   £30 for debtors, felons, and the bridewell. Three
guineas for travelling charges to quarter feſſions, to
report the ſtate of the health of the priſoners.

THIS goal, built about twenty years ago, is in an airy
healthy ſituation.—The *debtors* court and ward very properly ſeparate from thoſe for felons, but not from the
bridewell. The debtors floors are tarras, not eaſily
waſhed. The windows in general too ſmall and cloſe
glazed.—The *bridewell*, in the debtors court, has a large
work-room, a lodging-room for men, and two for women.—In the *felons* court there is for men a day room,
and down 3 ſteps a dungeon, $23\frac{1}{2}$ feet diameter : For women a day-room, and two ſmall night-rooms ; the latter
are too cloſe, $7\frac{1}{2}$ feet ſquare. The act for preſerving the
health of priſoners hung up. A neat chapel, but the ceiling too low : A new bath ; priſoners waſh in it before
aſſize and quarter ſeſſions : A copper juſt by to warm the
water.—Above are two rooms for an infirmary. There
is alſo a new room or parlour at the keeper's houſe, with
windows to the felons court : This circumſtance keeps
them quiet and orderly. The county allows eight guineas
a year for ſtraw.

A perſon goes round the county about Chriſtmas to gentlemen's houſes, and begs for the debtors. He carries a
                                                        book,

book, in which the giver enters his name, and donation. The whole amount, generally about £14.

DERBY TOWN GAOL

Is alfo the bridewell. Two rooms for debtors; one for felons; three for petty offenders. Prifoners always locked up: The narrow court or paffage, only 34 feet by 7, not being fecure, is of little ufe but for the keeper's fowls. The whole dirty and offenfive. Gaoler has a garden behind the prifon. No falary as gaoler; as keeper of bridewell, £5. Fees, debtors, 6s. 8d. felons 3s. 6d. No table. Garnifh 3s. 6d. on a paper in the debtors kitchen. Allowance to felons, one fhilling and fixpence weekly in bread. Licence for beer.

COUNTY GAOL at NOTTINGHAM.

GAOLER,   *Richard Eonington.*
   Salary,   £20.

   Fees,   Debtors,   } £0 - 14 - 8.
           Felons,   }

   Tranfports,   £7 - 17 - 6 each.
   Licence,   Beer.

PRISONERS,
   Allowance,   Debtors, three-halfpennyworth of bread a day.
            Felons, three halfpennyworth of bread and a halfpenny in money every day *(weight of threepenny loaf in Jan.* 1775, 1*lb.* 14 and a half *ounces.)*
   Garnifh,   prohibited.

CHAPLAIN,   Rev. Mr *Anderfon.*
   Duty,   Sunday and Wednefday.
   Salary,   £50.

SURGEON,   Mr *Bettefon,* now Mr *Partridge.*
   Salary,   £20, now 30, for debtors and felons.

THE gaol is on the fide of a hill. For mafter's-fide debtors only three rooms. Down 28 fteps are three rooms for criminals who can pay. Down 12 fteps more are deep dungeons, cut in the fandy rock, very damp: One of which is 23 feet by 13, and 7 feet high : Another, nearly circular, is about 12 feet diameter : The ftraw on barrack beds.

At my laft vifit, the felons court was more airy, the wall being palifaded ; and there was an entire feparation of debtors and felons.

For bathing here is (not, as in moft other county gaols, an inconvenient and almoft ufelefs tub—but) a large and very commodious bath, fupplied with river water ; and a copper juft by, to warm it when neceffary. This bath is a late improvement; and fo is the infirmary, near it, which has two rooms. The act for preferving the health of prifoners is neatly painted over the keeper's door. The juftices have allowed the gaoler to fupply the fick with better nourifhment, &c. to the amount of feven fhillings a week. Gentlemen fo remarkably confiderate and humane will, I hope, abolifh the unwholefome dungeons.

NOTTINGHAM TOWN AND COUNTY GAOL.

G A O L E R,	*Richard Bonington,* the county gaoler.
Salary,	£8.
Fees,	Debtors, £0 - 8 - 0 if under £10.
	0 - 14 - 8 if from any court in London.
	Felons, 0 - 14 - 8.
Tranfports,	7 - 17 - 6 each.
Licence,	*See County Gaol.*
P R I S O N E R S,	
Allowance,	Debtors, none.
	Felons, three-halfpence in bread, a day.
Garnifh,	lately prohibited.
C H A P L A I N,	None.
S U R G E O N,	None ftated. The mayor orders one when wanted.

THIS

THIS gaol has been lately repaired and much improved. Three rooms on the ground floor, two chambers, and two garrets : A dungeon down twenty-two steps, which I was informed has not been used for some years : A back court well supplied with water. Debtors have from a legacy one shilling a week for coals. Collected in the town for prisoners about four or five pounds a year.

A table of fees was hung up, dated the 10th of April 1777, signed by *Tho. Sands*, Mayor, *Rich. Butler*, and *John Fellows*, Aldermen, and confirmed by *W. H. Ashurst*, similar to that in county gaol.

COUNTY GAOL, LINCOLN CASTLE.

GAOLER, *Isaac Wood.*
    Salary, none. But £154 a year to supply prisoners as below ; and to pay land-tax &c.

Fees, Debtors, } £0 - 14 - 4.
        Felons, }

    Transports, £8 - 8 - 0 for each : And 13s. 4d. He paid the clerk of assize a guinea for each.
    Licence, Beer : Which the gaoler brews. He lets the Tap.

PRISONERS,
    Allowance, Debtors, the same as felons.
        Felons, each weekly 8lb. bread, and 2d. for beef : In common yearly £2, for coals : £2, straw : And £2, oatmeal.
    Garnish, £0 - 2 - 6.

CHAPLAINS, Rev. Mr *Simpson* : and Dr *Waldgrave* by his curate the Rev. Mr *Welling.*
    Duty, Mr *Simpson* Wednesday and Friday ; Mr *Welling* Sunday.
    Salary, Mr *Simpson* £5 &c. Dr *Waldgrave* about £35 *per* legacy of *Rebecca Hussey.*

SURGEON, Mr *Parnell.*
    Salary, £20.

THE

THE caftle belongs to the duchy of Lancafter. The county pays ten fhillings a year. The gaoler, *per con-tract*, to keep it in repair. A fpacious area of fix or feven acres. On the ground floor are the gaoler's apartments, the tap-room &c.

For mafter's-fide debtors, fix fizeable rooms on the firft ftory; and as many garrets. The floors of both ftories are tarras, and cannot be kept clean: The paffages only fix feet wide, with windows clofe glazed.

LINCOLN CITY AND COUNTY GAOL.

GAOLER,   *Francis Toyn.*
   Salary,   £20.

   Fees,   Debtors, } £0 - 6 - 8.
              Felons, }

   Tranfports, £10 each.
   Licence,   Beer.

PRISONERS,
   Allowance, Debtors, none.
            Felons, one fhilling a week.
   Garnifh,   One fhilling.
CHAPLAIN, None.

SURGEON, None.

THIS gaol, at the Stone-bow gate, has one large room for men-debtors, one fmaller for women, both up ftairs: In each a fire-place. The rooms for criminals are two dungeons down three fteps; with bedfteads, that they may not fleep on the damp earth floor. In one of them is a cage for clofer confinement when neceffary. Thefe prifoners are fometimes taken into the keeper's houfe. No court: No water acceffible to prifoners: No ftraw. The act for preferving the health of prifoners not hung up.

STAM-

S T A M F O R D   T O W N   G A O L.

THE gate which was the old prifon is taken down, and a new prifon is built at the town-hall. One good room for debtors in the keeper's houfe: For other prifoners two cells, 12 feet by 8: The window in each only 2 feet by 5 inches: And a bridewell-room 16 feet by 8: The window here alfo two fmall, 2 feet by 1 foot 8 inches.

Allowance to felons, two pence a day. Salary, as gaoler, £4; as keeper, £3 - 6 - 8. Which, though not figned, I tranfcribe for the fingularity of an article or two.

C O U N T Y   G A O L   AT   O A K H A M.

GAOLER,	*William Lumley*, now *Henry Lumley.*
Salary,	None.
Fees,	Debtors, } £0 - 14 - 10.
	Felons, }
Tranfports,	£10 each.
Licence,	Beer.

PRISONERS,

Allowance,	Debtors, } two fix-penny loaves a week.
	Felons, }
Garnifh,	One fhilling.
CHAPLAIN,	None.
SURGEON,	Mr *Bullivant*, now Mr *Berry.*
Salary,	£5 - 5 - 0.

THIS is alfo the county bridewell and the town gaol; yet I found it twice empty. On the ground floor is a day-room or kitchen for debtors:—A day-room, and two fmall night-rooms for felons; one of which being very fmall and quite clofe, the gaoler has made apertures in the door,

one

one at top, the other at bottom :—And a large work-room. The whole prifon is thatched.

N O R T H A M P T O N S H I R E.

COUNTY GAOL AT NORTHAMPTON.

GAOLER, *John Scofield.*
    Salary, *Now* £30. He pays the county £40 a year.

    Fees, Debtors, ⎱ £0 - 15 - 0.
            Felons, ⎰

    Tranfports, If two £7 each ; if more, £6 - 16 - 6.
    Licence, Beer and Wine.

PRISONERS,
    Allowance, Debtors, none.
            Felons, two penny-worth of bread a day, *(weight Jan.* 1775, 1*lb.* 1 and a-half *ounce.)* and *now* two pence for meat.
    Garnifh, Debtors, £0 - 6 - 0.
            Felons, 0 - 2 - 6.

CHAPLAIN, Rev. Mr *Miller.*
    Duty, Sunday, Tuefday, Thurfday.
    Salary, £40.

SURGEON, Mr *Kerr.* ⎱ Salary, none.
APOTHECARY, Mr *Breton.* ⎰ They make a bill.

THIS gaol is alfo the county bridewell ; but petty offen-ders are kept feparate from felons. Mr Scofield had a falary of £36 - 10 - 0 as keeper, and *now* as gaoler he has £30 added. Two courts ; but that for felons is too clofe. No ftraw. The county have built feven commo-dious rooms, for one felon each : Yet there are ftill two dungeons 11 fteps under ground. The gaol was clean, and the gaoler attentive and humane to his prifoners. Debtors, felons, and petty offenders were at work, fpin-ning ; making pegs for fhoemakers &c.

BERK-

COUNTY GAOL at READING.

GAOLER,   The Widow *Wiseman*; after her *John Hill*; now his widow.

Salary,   £20.
Fees,   Debtors, £0 - 16 - 10.
         Felons,   0 - 14 - 4.
Transports, £2 - 2 - 0 each.
Licence,   Beer and Wine.

PRISONERS,
Allowance,   Debtors, none.
         Felons,   three pence a day each,
Garnish,   Debtors, £0 - 5 - 6.
         Felons,   0 - 2 - 6.

CHAPLAIN,   Rev. Mr *Webster*.
Duty,   Sunday and Wednesday.
Salary,   £31 - 10 - 0.

SURGEON,   Mr *Tylleard*.
Salary,   £10 for gaol and bridewell.

READING.

DEBTORS and felons have their courts separated by iron rails. The former have a kitchen: And for the master's-side many rooms; but no free ward. Felons have a day-room for men and women. The night-room for men is a large dungeon down four steps: The prisoners broke out lately. A separate night-room for women. The turnkey has now a lodging-room, over the felons dungeon, with an alarm-bell; so that an escape will be more difficult. There is lately fitted up a small room for an infirmary; and another room or two: But no provision made for separating men-felons at night; nor for common-side debtors. There is a room used for the gaoler's poultry. Transports had not the king's allowance of 2s. 6d. a week. No table of fees. Clauses against spirituous liquors not hung up. No straw. The common-side debtors pay

P   1s.

1s. 6d. and the mafter's fide 2s. 6d. a week for lodging. The chapel is much too fmall.—I obferved at my laft vifit, that the act for preferving the health of prifoners was painted on a board in the debtors court.

COUNTY GAOL, OXFORD CASTLE.

G A O L E R,	*Solomon Wifdom.*	
Salary,	£.20.	
Fees,	Debtors, 1. 0 - 9 - 2.	
	Felons, 0 - 15 - 10.	
Tranfports,	He made a bill of the expence.	
Licence,	Beer and Wine.	

P R I S O N E R S,		
Allowance,	Debtors, none.	
	Felons, 16d. each *per* week in bread.	
Garnifh,	Lately cancelled.	

C H A P L A I N,	Rev. Mr *Swinton*, now Rev. Mr *Cotton*.	
Duty,	Sunday, Wednefday, Friday; the facrament four times a year.	
Salary,	l. 50, now l. 40.	

S U R G E O N,	Mr *Rawlins*.	
Salary,	l. 25 for felons.	

For the caftle gaol the county pays £40 a year to Mr Etty, who holds it of Chrift Church college on leafe. *Debtors* apartments fmall; and not enough of them for the general number of prifoners. No free ward: For lodging even in the tower *on their own beds* they muft pay 1s. 6d. a week: Their court is too fmall. Felons day-room or hall for men and women down 5 fteps, 21 feet by 15: The men's dungeon down 5 more; only a fmall window. The womens night room $6\frac{1}{2}$ feet by 4; no window. The court common to both, 29 feet by 23. The gaoler has a fpacious garden.

Since the north-gate was taken down, this prifon has been alfo the city gaol: For which Mr Wifdom has 5l. a year.—In 1773, eleven died of the fmall pox. In 1774,

that

that diftemper ftill in the gaol : In 1775, one debtor died of it in May ; three debtors and a petty offender in June : Three recovered. No infirmary : No ftraw. The act for preferving the health of prifoners not hung up.

COUNTY GAOL, WORCESTER CASTLE.

GAOLER,	*William Crane*, now his Widow.
Salary,	None.
Fees,	Debtors, l. o - 9 - 2.
	Felons, o - 15 - 10.
Tranfports,	No benefit to the gaoler. Clerk of the peace contracted with the merchants.
Licence,	Beer.
PRISONERS,	
Allowance,	Debtors, none.
	Felons, three-pennyworth of bread a day each.
Garnifh,	l. o - 2 - 6.
CHAPLAIN,	Rev. Mr *Taylor*.
Duty,	Friday.
Salary,	2ol.
SURGEON,	Mr *Hallward*.
Salary,	None : He makes a bill.

THE caftle-yard is fpacious : County members are chofen in it. In the gaoler's houfe are many good lodging-rooms for mafter's-fide debtors ; and two fmall day-rooms ; one of which is for common-fide debtors : One of thefe was ufed, at my former vifits, as a chapel; but now there is fitted up a larger and more convenient room for that purpofe. The free ward, or night-room for debtors, is at another part of the yard. The way to it is through the women-felons night-room. The day-room for men and women-felons is in the middle of the area ; only 14 feet by 12. Near it is a hand-ventilator for airing the men-felons dungeon, which is 26 fteps under ground, and circular, 18 feet diameter, with barrack bedfteads. Over it is an aperture in the court, with an iron grate. The felons work the ventilator cheerfully about a quarter of an hour before

P 2   they

they go down, and as long when they come up; for it
freſhens and cools the dungeon amazingly: We could
hardly keep our candle burning below while it was working. Excellent water at a pump in the yard.

WORCESTER CITY and COUNTY GAOL.

GAOLER,   *Richard George,* now his Widow.
   Salary,   None.
   Fees,   Debtors, l. o - 9 - 2.
          Felons,   o - 5 - o.
   Tranſports,   No benefit to the gaoler.
   Licence,   Beer.

PRISONERS,
   Allowance.   Debtors, none.
          Felons,   three pence a day each.
   Garniſh,   l. o - 2 - 6.

CHAPLAIN, None.

SURGEON,   Mr *Hallward.*
   Salary,   None: He makes a bill.

THIS is alſo the city bridewell. The debtors free ward
is ſpacious. Only one day-room for criminals: One common court: Another might be taken from the keeper's
large garden. At my former viſits he paid window-tax;
which he ſaid brought him under the diſagreeable neceſſity
of ſtopping up ſome windows; but this is now taken off.
Clauſes againſt ſpirituous liquors not hung up. As to
cleanlineſs, I found this a contraſt to the priſon juſt mentioned.

COUNTY GAOL at STAFFORD,

GAOLER,   *William Scott.*
   Salary,   None.
   Fees,   Debtors, l. o - 17 - 4.
          Felons,   o - 15 - 10.
   Tranſports,   6l. each.
   Licence.   Beer and Wine.

PRISONERS,

PRISONERS,

Allowance,	Debtors, Felons,	} each *per* week, 15*d.* bread, and 9*d.* cheefe ; and for the felons 3 *Cwt* of coals a week from Michaelmas to May-day.
Garnifh,	Debtors,	l. o - 2 - 1½
	Felons,	cancelled by the gaoler.

CHAPLAIN,	Rev. Mr *Unett.*
Duty,	Sunday, Wednefday, Friday ; a fermon once in about two months.
Salary,	lately augmented from 20l. to 30l.
SURGEON,	Mr *Ward,* now Mr *Richard Hughes.*
Salary,	20l.

This gaol is too fmall for the number of prifoners.
The debtors court and free ward are fpacious. In the
latter is a *hand-ventilator* for the men-felons dungeon
which is under it ; but being out of repair, has not been
ufed for fome years. Were the county to allow the fmall
fum of a guinea a year, it might always be kept in order,
as is done in Worcefter-caftle. An alarm bell in this
crowded gaol would be very proper.—One fmall day-
room for men and women-felons, down 3 fteps. The
dungeon where the men-felons fleep is very clofe, having
no window, and is about 2 feet below the paffage. The
felons court is alfo too fmall. It is pity that the ftream
juft on the outfide of the walls is not within them. I was
pleafed to fee plenty of clean *ftraw* in both dungeons ;
and found it was owing to the generous and exemplary
practice of *not farming it,* but allowing the gaoler to order
it whenever wanted, and the county paying for it *themfelves.*
The chapel is fmall, and at the top of the houfe. No infirmary.

COUNTY GAOL AT SHREWSBURY.

GAOLER,	*Samuel Wilding.*
Salary,	None.
Fees,	Debtors, l. o - 9 - o.
	Felons, o - 14 - 4

Tran-

Tranfports,   l. 6 - 6 - o each.
Licence,   Beer and Wine.

PRISONERS,
  Allowance,   Debtors, two fix-penny loaves a week each.
                Felons,   1s. 4d.¼ in bread a week each.
  Garnifh,   Lately cancelled.

CHAPLAIN,   Rev. Mr *Humphreys*, now Rev. Mr *Rowland*.
  Duty,   Sunday and Thurfday.
  Salary,   35l.

SURGEON,   Mr *Cooper*.
  Salary,   None : He makes a bill.

APOTHECARY, Mr *James Winall*.
  Salary,   None : He makes a bill.

THIS prifon was built, as by date in the debtors court, 1705.—Separate courts for debtors and felons; but the latter have no water. For this reafon, and becaufe their day-room is in the debtors court, both debtors and felons are commonly together in that court. Commodious apartments for mafter's-fide debtors: And a large free ward for the common-fide. For felons there are two night-dungeons down 11 fteps: That for men was a few years ago made more airy by an additional window: And it is, or fhould be, daily frefhened by a hand-ventilator which is in the room over the chapel. The women's dungeon might alfo be frefhened by the fame. The day-room for felons is fmall, 15½ feet by 5½: Men and women together. The county has now enclofed a court for the women; but a feparate day-room is alfo neceffary to prevent the dreadful confequences of their being with the men. There fhould be water in this court; as alfo in that of the men-felons.

HERE-

HEREFORDSHIRE,

COUNTY GAOL AT HEREFORD.

GAOLER,   *Thomas Ireland.*
  Salary,   None.

  Fees,   Debtors, } l. o - 14 - 4.
            Felons, }

  Tranſports, l. 5 - 10 - 0. each.
  Licence, Beer.

PRISONERS,
  Allowance, Debtors, none.
            Felons, a three-penny loaf each, every other day.
  Garniſh, l. 0 - 2 - 6.

CHAPLAIN,   Rev. Mr *Baylis*; now Rev. Mr *Underwood.*
  Duty,   Sunday, Wedneſday, Friday, and ſaints days.
  Salary,   40l. Twenty of it is a legacy of William Bridges, Eſq; of Tiverton in this county.

SURGEON,   Mr *William Cam.*
  Salary,   15l.

HEREFORD.

Apartments, and court for maſter's-ſide debtors, ſpacious: But no free ward. The men-felons night-ward, the *Camp*, was too cloſe, but is lately made airy and commodious: Their court behind the gaol large. No infirmary: No ſtraw or bedding. The chapel was very damp, but it is now floored and dry. Clauſes againſt ſpirituous liquors, and act for preſerving the health of priſoners, not hung up. Mr Ireland, who has been there above forty years, ſaid, at one of my former viſits, he never had a debtor who obtained the groats.

HEREFORD CITY GAOL

Is one of the gates. The debtors rooms are commodious; and they have a little court. The lower room
for

for felons too clofe. The gaol clean, but out of repair.
Claufes of act againft fpirituous liquors not hung up.
Keeper a widow : Salary none : Fees, 6s. 8d. No table.

C O U N T Y   G A O L   AT   M O N M O U T H.

G A O L E R,	*John Daverel*, afterwards *James Baker*, now his Widow.
Salary,	None. 2ol. a year to fupply felons as below.
Fees,	Debtors, } l. 1 - 0 - 10. Felons, }
Tranfports,	6l. each.
Licence,	Beer.
P R I S O N E R S,	
Allowance,	Debtors, none. Felons, one-pennyworth of bread a day each.
Garnifh,	l. 0 - 2 - 6.
C H A P L A I N,	None.
S U R G E O N,	Mr *Powell*.
Salary,	l. 10 - 10 - 0, lately augmented to l. 12 - 12 - 0.

ONLY one court. The rooms for debtors fmall. Felons
night-room at top of the houfe, 22 feet by 15, with only
one window about 3 feet fquare. Befides the difficulty of
going daily up and down in irons ; when water is to be
carried fo high, and the ftaircafe, like this, is narrow and
inconvenient, a room is feldom clean and healthy. This
cannot be fo if it fhould be crowded. At my firft vifit in
1774, they had the gaol fever, of which J. Daverel and
feveral of his prifoners, and fome of their friends died.—
No infirmary : There is room to build one at the bottom
of the court. The brewhoufe is very fit for a felons day-
room ; which is much wanted.

After the mortality mentioned above, all the prifoners
were new-clothed by the duke of Beaufort.

COUNTY

COUNTY GAOL, GLOUCESTER CASTLE.

GAOLER,   *William Williams.*
   Salary,   None.
   Fees,   Debtors,   —   l. 1 - 0 - 10.
           Felons at Affize   0 - 17 - 8.
           ———at Quarter Seffions   0 - 13 - 4.
   Tranfports, 6l. each.
   Licence,   Beer.

PRISONERS,
   Allowance, Debtors, none.
           Felons,   each a fixpenny loaf in two days.
   Garnifh,   l. 0 - 1 - 6.

CHAPLAIN,   Rev. Mr *Evans.*
   Duty,   Sunday, Wednefday, Friday.
   Salary,   40l.
SURGEON,   None; but on applying to a juftice.

THE caftle is alfo one of the county bridewells: Yet only one court for all prifoners; and one fmall day-room, 12 feet by 11, for men and women-felons. The free ward for debtors is 19 feet by 11, which having no window, part of the plafter-wall is broke down for light and air. The night-room (the *Main*) for men-felons, though up many ftone fteps, is clofe and dark; and thefloor is fo ruinous that it cannot be wafhed. Adjoining to the *Main*, there are other night-rooms for fines, &c. Thefe have alfo their feparate day-room. The whole prifon is much out of repair. The upper rooms were the bridewell, but now they are not ufed. Many prifoners died here in 1773, and I generally faw fome fick in this gaol; eight died about Chriftmas 1778 of the fmall pox. No infirmary. Neither claufes againft fpirituous liquors, nor the act for preferving the health of prifoners, are hung up.

Q   GLOU.

GLOUCESTER CITY AND COUNTY GAOL.

GAOLER,   *William Jeynes,* now his Widow.
    Salary,   None : She pays l. 4 - 14 - 0 a year to the sheriffs.
    Fees,   Debtors, l. 0 - 9 - 8.
        Felons,   0 - 12 - 10.
    Transports, 6l. each.
    Licence,   Beer.

PRISONERS,
    Allowance, Debtors, three shillings a week.
            Felons,   three-pennyworth of bread a day each.
    Garnish,   l. 0 - 3 - 4.

CHAPLAIN,   None.

SURGEON,   None ; but on applying to the mayor.

THIS gaol, the North-gate, is too small. Debtors, felons, and petty offenders, who cannot pay for beds, all together in the *Main ;* but women separated at night. No court; debtors have the privilege of walking upon the leads. The act for preserving the health of prisoners not hung up.

HAMPSHIRE, OR THE COUNTY OF SOUTHAMPTON.

COUNTY GAOL AT WINCHESTER.

GAOLER,   *John White.*
    Salary,   None.
    Fees,   Debtors, l. 1 - 0 - 0.
        Felons,   1 - 7 - 4.
    Transports, l. 5 - 5 - 0 each, and hire of waggon or other
        carriage.
    Licence,   Beer and Wine.

PRISONERS,
    Allowance, Debtors, none ; but on applying to the justices.
            Felons,   a three-penny loaf each, every other
                day *(weight in Sept.* 1774, 1*lb.* 15*oz.)*
                and the college allowance.
    Garnish,   l. 0 - 2 - 6.

CHAP-

CHAPLAIN,   Rev. Mr *Weſtcomb*.
   Duty,   Sunday, Tueſday, Thurſday.
   Salary,   Lately augmented from l. 30 to 50.

SURGEON,   Mr *Lipſcomb*.
   Salary,   Lately augmented from l. 30 to 50 for felons, com-
       mon-ſide debtors, and bridewell priſoners.

THIS gaol is kept very clean; and the alterations in it are improvements. The preſent dungeon, 48 feet by 23, is down but 5 ſteps: It is boarded, and has 3 large windows. The former deſtructive dungeon was darker, and down 11 ſteps: Mr Lipſcomb informed me that more than 20 priſoners had died in it of the *gaol fever* in one year; and that his predeceſſor died of the ſame diſtemper. The felons day-room is commodiouſly enlarged. Their ſtraw mattreſſes and coverlets are brought out and aired when the weather is fine. The beds are all on crib bed-ſteads. They had every day a clean towel hung on a roller: The priſoner who took care of it and delivered it next day was paid a penny. If a little court, which is now ſhut up from the gaol, and totally uſeleſs, were cleared, and opened towards the priſon, it would be very conducive to health and convenience. The chapel is very low and inconvenient.

PORTSMOUTH TOWN GAOL.

In one of the rooms, which is large, debtors and felons formerly lodged together; but in 1779, I found that they were ſeparated. The upper rooms are for women: None in them. Gaoler is ſergeant at mace: No ſalary: Licence for beer and wine. Priſoners allowance, debtors none; felons four pence a day. No bedding nor ſtraw.

A table of fees is hung up in this gaol: It is ſigned by the town-clerk George Huiſh 30th June 1736. He writes

Q 2   at

at the title, " Fees due to the fergeants at mace of the
" faid borough, which I have known to be paid from the
" year 1693 and have been informed were antiently paid."

COUNTY GAOL at SALISBURY.

GAOLER,   *Thomas Biggs.*
     Salary,   None. But 8ol. a year (lately raifed from 5ol.)
       to fupply felons as below.
     Fees,   Debtors, l. 1 - 1 - 0.
      Felons,   1 - 6 - 4.
   Tranfports, l. 4 - 4 - 0 each.
   Licence,   Beer and Wine.

PRISONERS,
     Allowance, Debtors, none.
      Felons, a penny loaf a day each *(weight in Sept.*
       1774, 8 oz.)*; now 2d. a day; i. e.
       $1\frac{1}{2}d.$ bread, $\frac{1}{2}d.$ a quart fmall beer.
     Garnifh,   Debtors Mafter's-fide,   —   l. 0 - 8 - 3
       Felons and common-fide Debtors,   0 - 4 - 4

CHAPLAIN,   Rev. Mr *Vanderplank.*
     Duty,   Friday only.
     Salary,   4ol. of which 2ol. is a legacy.

SURGEON,   Mr *Crompton,* now Mr *Curtoys.*
     Salary,   l. 10 - 10 - 0 for felons and common-fide debtors,
      now 21l.

THE prifon in this city called *Fifherton-Anger Gaol*
(from the name of the parifh in which it ftands) near a
fine ftream is alfo one of the county bridewells. Only
one court. No day-room for common-fide debtors, nor
felons: Each fort have their fire on a brick hearth raifed
in the middle of their refpective lodging rooms, without
a chimney. The debtors room over the felons. Women-felons have a feparate room, more commodious.

                    COUNTY

COUNTY GAOL at DORCHESTER.

GAOLER,   *James Chaffey.*
Salary,   None.
Fees,   Debtors,   —   l. 1 - 3 - 9.
            Felons at Affize,   —   1 - 3 - 8.
            ————Quarter Seffions,   0 - 17 - 4.
Tranfports, l. 2 - 12 - 6 each.
Licence,   Beer.

PRISONERS,
Allowance, Debtors, none : but on applying to juftices.
           Felons, three-halfpennyworth of bread a day
                   (weight in Sept. 1774, 12½ *oz.)*
Garnifh,   Debtors. l. 0 - 2 - 7.
           Felons,   0 - 1 - 3.

CHAPLAIN, Rev. Mr *Dolney.*
Duty,   Friday ; altered lately to Sunday and Wednefday.
Salary,   Lately raifed from l. 30 to 50.

SURGEON, Mr *Kenn.*
Salary,   30l. for debtors and felons.

THIS gaol was out of repair, and dirty at my firft vifits, but is now cleaner. Only one court. In September 1774, two debtors told me they had lived five or fix weeks on nothing but the county bread, and water. In December 1775, the fmall pox in the gaol : No infirmary. A garden and a fine ftream at the back of the gaol. Claufes againft fpirituous liquors, and the act for preferving the health of prifoners, are not hung up.

HIGH GAOL at EXETER,

FOR FELONS.

GAOLER,   *Benjamin Sherry.*
Salary,   None.
Fees,   Felons, l. 0 - 14 - 4.
Tranfports, l. 1 - 1 - 0 each.
Licence,   He fells beer.

PRISONERS,

PRISONERS,
    Allowance, Felons, twenty-two ounces of bread a day each.
    Garnish.   Lately abolished.

CHAPLAIN,   Rev. Mr *Stobbock*.
    Duty,   Sunday a sermon, and twice a week prayers.
    Salary,   40l.

SURGEON,   Mr *Rule*. *(since dead)*.
    Salary,   42l. for gaol and bridewell.

THIS gaol is the property of John Rolle Walter, Efq; whose family had a grant of it from the duchy of Cornwall: The gaoler pays him rent £22 *per annum*. The house and court too small: No fewer. The three night-dungeons down 3 steps are close and unhealthy: The windows too small. An infirmary, commodious enough, is lately built; but the stairs that lead up to it are intolerably bad. The prisoners formerly made cabbage nets for two pence a dozen, and purses of different sorts from four pence to seven pence a dozen: The turnkey found the twine and thread. Two sailors fined a shilling each had £1 - 1 - 4 each to pay the clerk of the peace, besides the gaoler's fees. Mr Rule the surgeon told me that he was by contract excused from attending in the dungeons any prisoners that should have the gaol fever.

SHERIFF's WARD, EXETER;

THE COUNTY PRISON FOR DEBTORS.

KEEPER,   *John Jutsum*.
    Salary,   None.

    Fees   l. 0 - 14 - 4.
    Licence, Beer.

PRISONERS,
    Allowance, None.
    Garnish, None.

CHAPLAIN,   None. On Sunday a prifoner reads prayers and dines with the keeper.

SURGEON,   None.

THE Sheriff's ward or prifon is in the parifh of St Thomas the apoftle, in the county of Devon. The rooms are large and convenient, but out of repair. Court fpacious. Good rules of œconomy. A humane keeper. He has a good fire for common-fide debtors—he faid he would gladly relinquifh his fees for a falary of £100—and told me that during his time, about twelve years, no more than four or five debtors had obtained their aliment, *the groats.* One debtor, on attachment from the court of chancery, has continued here from May 1758, who would not take the benefit of the infolvent acts.

EXETER CITY AND COUNTY GAOL.

GAOLER,   *Sarah Strong.*
  Salary,   20l.
  Fees,   Debtors, l. 0 - 16 - 4.
          Felons,   0 - 14 - 4.
  Tranfports, The expence.
  Licence,   Beer.

PRISONERS,
  Allowance, Debtors, none.
          Felons,   three-halfpennyworth of bread a day each.
  Garnifh,   Debtors, l. 0 - 3 - 6.

CHAPLAIN,   None.

SURGEON,   None. But ordered for felons by the chamber upon occafion.

THIS gaol, called the *South-gate Prifon,* has in the keeper's houfe convenient apartments for *debtors.* The
three

three wards on the other fide of the gateway, for felons, are very clofe and offenfive: No chimney: No court: No water: No fewer. In 1779, I found a woman fick, who had been confined three years on the felons fide. The act for preferving the health of prifoners not hung up.

PLYMOUTH TOWN GAOL.

Two rooms for felons; and a large room above for debtors. One of the former, the *Clink*, 17 feet by 8, about 5½ feet high, with a wicket in the door 7 inches by 5 to admit light and air. To this, as I was informed, three men who were confined near two months under fentence of tranfportation, came by turns for breath. The door had not been opened for five weeks when I with difficulty entered to fee a pale inhabitant. He had been there ten weeks under fentence of tranfportation, and faid he had much rather have been hanged than confined in that noifome cell. No court: No water: No fewer. The gaolers live diftant; they are the three ferjeants at mace. Fees, 15s. 10d. No table. Allowance to debtors, none but on application: Felons, two-pennyworth of bread a day. No ftraw.

COUNTY GAOL AT LAUNCESTON,

FOR FELONS.

G A O L E R,	*John Mules*, deputy, under *Coryndon Carpenter* Efq; conftable of the caftle *(fince dead)*.
Salary,	Lately augmented by the county from l. 8 to 12.
Fees.	Felons, l. 0 - 16 - 8.
Tranfports,	4d. a mile each.
Licence,	None.

PRISON-

PRISONERS,
Allowance, Felons, a three-penny loaf each in two days; white or brown at their option *(weight in Dec. 1775, of white bread* 1lb. 10oz. *brown,* 2lb. 2oz*)*.

CHAPLAIN, Rev. Mr *Lethbridge.*
Duty, Tuefday and Friday.
Salary, 50l.

SURGEON, Mr *Bennet.*
Salary, 15l.

THIS gaol, though built in a large green belonging to the old ruinous caftle, is very fmall; houfe and court meafuring only 52 feet by 44; and the houfe not covering half that ground. The prifon is a room or paffage 23½ feet by 7½, with only one window 2 feet by 1½: And three dungeons or cages on the fide oppofite the window: Thefe are about 6½ feet deep; one 9 feet long; one about 8; one not 5: This laft for women. They are all very offenfive. No chimney: No water: No fewers: Damp earth floors: No infirmary. The court not fecure; and prifoners feldom permitted to go out to it. Indeed the whole prifon is out of repair, and yet the gaoler lives dif-tant. I once found the prifoners chained two or three to-gether. Their provifion was put down to them through a hole (9 inches by 8) in the floor of the room above (ufed as a chapel); and thofe who ferved them there, often caught the fatal fever. At my firft vifit I found the keeper, his affiftant, and all the prifoners but one fick of it: And heard that a few years before, many prifoners had died of it; and the keeper and his wife in one night.

I learned th. t a woman who was difcharged juft before my firft vifit (by the grand jury making a collection for her fees) had been confined three years by the ecclefiaftical court, and had three children in the gaol. There is no table of fees.

Q   SHERIFF's

SHERIFF's WARD at BODMIN,

The COUNTY PRISON for Debtors.

KEEPER, *Joseph Gatty*, now his Widow.
  Salary,   25l.
  Fees,   Debtors, l. 0 - 13 - 4,
             besides   0 - 4 - 1 to the sheriff.
  Licence,   Of late none.

PRISONERS,
  Allowance, None.
  Garnish,   l. 0 - 2 - 0.

CHAPLAIN, None.

SURGEON, None.

THIS prison, for which the sheriff pays 20l. a year, is out of repair. A spacious back court; with a stream running through it. The keeper pays window-tax l. 3 - 7 - 0; and some windows were stopped up. He said he had been in that office above twenty years; and during the whole time had but four prisoners who obtained from their creditors the allowance commonly called the *groats*.

COUNTY GAOL at IVELCHESTER.

GAOLER,   *Edward Scadding.*
  Salary.   25l.
  Fees,   Debtors, l. 0 - 14 - 4.
              Felons,   0 - 6 - 8.
  Transports, l. 3 - 12 - 0 each.
  Licence,   Beer and Wine.

PRISONERS,
  Allowance, Debtors, none.
              Felons, two pence a day each, money; lately
                altered to the value in standard-bread.
  Garnish,   l. 0 - 3 - 6.

CHAPLAIN, Rev. Mr *Dumett*, now Rev. Mr *Pester.*
  Duty,   Sunday, Wednesday, Friday.
  Salary,   50l.

SURGEON,

S U R G E O N,   Mr *Shorland*.
Salary,   8l.

THE gaol is near the river, and has no offenfive fewers. The apartments roomy ; but the courts too little. They might be enlarged eaftward. Women-felons have no day-room : A room, which is fit, and feems to have been defigned for that ufe, is taken by the gaoler for a ftable. Affizes never held here. Prifoners are removed for trial to the bridewell at Taunton ; or to Bridgewater, where the prifon is only one room ; or to Wells, where there is no prifon at all : And yet, at Midfummer affize 1775, the prifoners were kept in that city eight days. The act for preferving the health of prifoners not hung up.

BRISTOL CITY AND COUNTY GAOL.

G A O L E R,   *Henry Williams*, now *William Driver*.
Salary,   None. Gown-money 2l. a year.
Fees,   Debtors, l. 0 - 6 - 8.
    Felons,   0 - 13 - 4.
Tranfports,   l. 5 - 5 - 0 each.
Licence,   Beer,

P R I S O N E R S,
Allowance,   Debtors, none.
    Felons, a pennyworth of bread a day, before trial; two-pennyworth of bread after conviction.
Garnifh,   l. 0 - 2 - 7.

C H A P L A I N,   Rev. Mr *Eafterbrook*.
Duty,   Sunday, Wednefday, Friday.
Salary,   36l.

S U R G E O N,   Mr *Abel Dagge (fince dead.)*
Salary,   None : He makes a bill.

BRISTOL NEWGATE.

THIS Newgate (as that in the metropolis) ftands in the midft of the city. It is too fmall for the general number

of prifoners.   For debtors there are about fifteen rooms ;
yet no free ward.   The pooreft pay ten pence halfpenny
a week : Others two fhillings and fixpence.   For women-
felons, a day-room and feveral night-rooms.   For men-
felons, a day-room, with a court yard adjacent 20 feet by
12.   Their dungeon, the *Pit*, down 18 fteps, is 17 feet
diameter, and 9 feet high : Barrack bedfteads : No bedding nor ftraw.   It is clofe and offenfive : Only a fmall
window.   There is another yard, the *Tennis Court*, larger
than that of the felons : Prifoners are admitted into it by
turns.   A room or two at the top of the houfe for an infirmary.   There are many narrow paffages : The utmoft attention is requifite to keep the prifon healthy.   I found it
clean ; confidering it was fo crowded and fo clofe.   It
was fcraped and lime-whited once a year before the late
act for preferving the health of prifoners.   That act is
neatly painted on a board hung up in the chapel, which is
commodious and has a gallery : feveral texts of fcripture
are painted in fundry parts of it.—Claufes againft fpirituous liquors are not hung up.   No table of gaoler's fees.

BATH CITY GAOL.

THE afcent to this prifon, built in a meadow which is
fometimes overflowed, is by a fine flight of ftone fteps.
On the ground floor is the keeper's kitchen, &c. and fome
rooms for petty offenders.   Above are three ftories ; five
rooms on each : One or two of them ufed by the keeper :
The reft for debtors ; one bed in a room, in which if two
prifoners fleep, they pay two fhillings a week each ; if one
has it to himfelf, he pays two fhillings and fix pence a
week.   Two rooms on the fecond ftory are free wards ;
on the upper floors is their work-fhop.   There is a court
with offenfive fewers too near the houfe.—Keeper, a fheriff's

riff's officer : No falary : Fees, if from the court of requefts: 3s 6d. thefe debtors are cleared in thirteen weeks,
paying thofe fees : Debtors for large fums, 7s. 8d. No
table. Licence for beer. Allowance, to debtors, none :
To offenders, 2d. a day : No ftraw. Claufes againft fpirituous liquors, and the act for preferving the health of
prifoners, not hung up.—No chaplain, nor furgeon.

COUNTY GAOL, YORK CASTLE.

GAOLER,   *Thomas Wharton,* now *William Clayton.*
   Salary,   None.
   Fees,   Debtors, l. 0 - 8 - 8.
           Felons, 0 - 9 - 6.
           Admiffion, 0 - 3 - 4.
   Tranfports,   —   10 - 10 - 0 each.
   Licence,   Beer and Wine.

PRISONERS,
   Allowance, Debtors, certified by their parifh, } a fix-penny loaf
               Felons, — —   each on
                Tuefday and Friday *(weight Nov.* 1774,
                3lb. 2oz.)
   Garnifh,   Cancelled in 1774.

CHAPLAINS, Rev. Mr *Peacock,* and Rev. Mr *Bridges.*
   Duty,   Mr *Peacock* Monday, Tuefday, Wednefday, Thurfday;
           and from Lady-day to Michaelmas, Sunday. Mr
           Bridges a fermon.
   Salary,   Mr *Peacock* 5ol. from the county ; Mr *Bridges* 25l.
           from a legacy. Not in the lift.

SURGEON,   Mr *Stilingfleet,* now Mr *Favell.*
   Salary,   4ol. for debtors and felons.

IN the fpacious area is a noble prifon for debtors, which
does honour to the county. You afcend by a fine flight
of ftone fteps to a floor on which are 11 rooms, full 16
feet fquare, near 12 feet high. Above them is the fame
number of rooms : One or two of thefe for common-fide
debtors. The rooms are airy and healthy. The debtors
                                 weave

weave confiderable quantities of garters, purfes, laces, &c.
On the ground floor are the gaoler's apartments, &c.

The felons court is down 5 fteps: It is too fmall, and
has no water: The pump is juft on the outfide of the
palifades. The day-room for men is only 24 feet by
8: In it are three cells: In another place nine cells: And
three in another. The cells are in general about $7\frac{1}{2}$ feet
by $6\frac{1}{2}$, and $8\frac{1}{2}$ high; clofe and dark; having only
either a hole over the door about 4 inches by 8, or fome
perforations in the door of above an inch diameter: Not
any of them into the open air, but into paffages or entries.
In moft of thefe cells three prifoners are locked up at
night; in winter for fourteen to fixteen hours: Straw on
the ftone floors; no bedfteads. There are four condemned rooms about 7 feet fquare. A fewer in one of the paffages often makes thefe parts of the gaol very offenfive:
and I cannot fay they are clean. Indeed a clean prifon
is fcarcely ever feen, where the water is to be brought in
by the gaoler's fervants. The next houfe to the caftle-
gate, and others in the neighbourhood, have river-water
laid in at a moderate expence.

Women-felons are kept quite feparate: They have two
courts, but no water: You go down four fteps to their
two clofe rooms, a day and a night-room. Their con-
demned-room is in another part of the gaol: Near it is a
room to confine debtors who do not behave well.

The infirmary near the gate is only one middle-fized
room. When prifoners of one fex are there, thofe of the
other are excluded: At one of my vifits a fick man was
kept out for that reafon.

At affize fome prifoners appear in court on their trial
in

in the county-clothing. The county pays Mr John Sherwood £.21 a year to infpect and weigh the bread, and deliver it to the prifoners. He conftantly attends for this purpofe on Tuefday and Friday. The gaoler is a fheriff's officer. Tranfports convicted at quarter feffions had, befides the bread allowance, one fhilling a week. Thofe caft at affize had the king's allowance of 2s. 6d. a week.

The grand fhire-hall in the caftle-yard is now finifhed. May it not be hoped the gentlemen of this great county will not ftop there, but proceed to build a proper prifon for felons, in which boys may be feparated from old offenders, and the other inconveniences of the prefent gaol avoided?—At my laft vifit, ground was marked out for an additional building, oppofite to the fhire-hall, that there might be a feparation of felons, and alfo rooms for the fick.

Yorkfhire. ORDERS and FEES fettled by the Juftices of the Peace of the feveral Ridings of the County of York and confirmed by the Juftice of Affize—which are to be obferved and kept by the gaoler—and all prifoners— until the fame fhall be legally altered.

	l.	s.	d.
Firft That every knight fhall pay for his weekly commons at table if he eats with them	0	13	4
For his fee if committed by warrant on a civil action	0	13	4
Every efquire for his commons at table weekly if he eats with them	0	10	4
For his fee if committed by warrant on a civil action	0	10	4
Every gentleman for his commons at table weekly if he eats with them	0	8	0
For his fee if committed by warrant on a civil action	0	8	0
Every yeoman, tradefman or artificer for his weekly commons at table if he eats with them	0	6	8
For his fee if committed by warrant on a civil action	0	3	4
And it is further ordered that every knight fhall pay nightly for his bed	0	0	6
Every efquire for the fame	0	0	6
Every gentleman for the fame	0	0	4
Every yeoman tradefman or artificer for the fame	0	0	2

And that when the gaoler lodgeth two or more prifoners in one bed they fhall pay for their lodgings amongft them after the rates above

And

	l.	*s.*	*d.*

And every prifoner who provides his own bed and bedding fhall have a room affigned fuitable to his or their quality and fhall pay nothing fer the fame

And that upon the difcharge of a debtor if there be feveral actions againft him the gaoler fhall take no more than one fee and that to be — — — — 0 6 8

And upon the difcharge of every debtor to the turnkeys and no more — — — — 0 2 0

And that every prifoner fhall have liberty to provide and fend for victuals drink and other neceffaries from any place whatfoever at all feafonable times for their own proper ufe only and not to fell the fame.

And every prifoner committed from the bar by the judge or judges of affize and gaol delivery in the affize week fhall pay for their commitment fee only — — — 0 2 0

And every perfon committed to the gaol for fufpicion of felony, or for mifdemeanor, if upon his or her trial he or fhe fhall be found not guilty and be thereupon difcharged, fhall pay to the gaoler for his difcharging fee — — 0 6 8

And to the turnkeys — — 0 2 0

And that every perfon convicted or attainted of felony or found guilty of a mifdemeanor which fhall be reprieved and difcharged by pardon fhall pay to the gaoler for his difcharging fee 0 7 6

And to the turnkey — — — 0 2 0

And every perfon that fhall appear upon recognizance for fufpicion of felony and is thereupon committed to gaol and fhall not be indicted but acquitted by proclamation, fhall be difcharged paying to the gaoler — — — 0 2 0

And all others that fhall be committed to gaol before the affizes or gaol delivery and fhall not be indicted but acquitted by proclamation be difcharged paying to the gaoler — 0 2 0

An Account of the CHARITY given to the Prifoners in his Majefty's Gaol the Caftle of York.

	l.	*s.*	*d.*

The Lady Lumley, to be given yearly on St Thomas's day and paid by the lord mayor of York — — 6 7 0

The honourable and ancient city of York weekly in bread 0 2 6

Mrs Frances Thornhill for ftraw, the lord mayor of York has 30l. in his hands for that purpofe — — 1 10 0

Dr Phineas Hodgefon paid weekly in rolls to all that hear fermons 0 2 0

Alderman White's bread by the name of Swain's bread, paid out of a clofe belonging to John Legg, quarterly 6s. 6d. — 1 6 0

Mr Bowes gave twenty fhillings to be paid quarterly in bread 1 0 0

Mrs Mary Lawfon of Micklegate in the city of York widow by will dated the 22d July 1729 gave 100l. for the difcharging of poor prifoners for debt out of the county gaol of York whofe debts did not exceed the fum of

· of 20l.—and her executrixes—Mrs Catherine Bower—and Mrs Ann Maxwell difcharged with faid money thirty two prifoners.

The right honourable Richard earl of Burlington and Sir George Savile Bart. gave each of them ten guineas for the like ufe—with which twenty guineas the Rev. Mr Kayley ordinary of the faid gaol difcharged eighteen prifoners.

COUNTY BRIDEWELLS.

WEST-RIDING, WAKEFIELD. This prifon is unfortunately built upon low ground; fo that it is damp, and expofed to floods. Four of the wards are fpacious; but all the wards are made very offenfive by fewers, which are dark. Prifon and court out of fight from the keeper's houfe, though adjoining; and fome prifoners have efcaped. They are now let out to the court only half an hour in the day. The wards are dirty: A prifon on ground fo low as this, requires the utmoft attention to cleanlinefs.—Keeper's falary lately raifed from 80l. to 105l. he contracting to fupply *ftraw* and *coals*. No fees. Allowance, two pence a day: Little or no employment. ——The infirmary is now finifhed, confifting of two good rooms, arched with brick, $21\frac{1}{4}$ feet by 17.

NORTH-RIDING, THIRSK. Six rooms on the ground floor, in one of them a chimney. The county has ground enough about this prifon to enlarge it, and feparate the men and women. If they do, they fhould think of an infirmary; for the keeper told me his prifoners had the gaol fever not long ago. His falary, l. 26 : 10 : 0. Fees, 2s. Claufes againft fpirituous liquors not hung up·

EAST-RIDING, BEVERLEY. On the ground floor three fmall night-rooms; and a new work-room with a chimney:

R

ney: Above, four rooms for thofe that pay. In the court not only a pump, but a ciftern of rain-water. Coals, two chaldron and a half a year. No ftraw. At my laft vifit I faw fome tile-fherds, which probably were defigned for employment. Keeper's falary, 30l. Fees, 4s. No table.

YORK CITY and COUNTY GAOL.

GAOLER,	*Quintin Ackam,* now *Francis Meggefon.*
Salary,	*Now* 10l. He pays l. 10 - 10 - 0 a year to the under-fheriff.
Fees,	Debtors, l. 0 - 6 - 8.
	Felons, 0 - 7 - 8.
Tranfports,	probably the fame as at the caftle.
Licence,	Beer and Wine.
PRISONERS,	
Allowance,	Debtors, none but legacies.
	Felons, of late, nine pence a week in bread.
Garnifh,	l. 0 - 7 - 0.
CHAPLAIN,	None.
SURGEON,	Mr *Wallis,* occafionally.

THIS gaol upon Oufe-bridge, called the *Kidcots,* has on one fide of the bridge four convenient chambers for debtors, about 11 feet fquare: For thefe they pay fix pence a week. Below them is a free ward with barrack-beds; and a room to the ftreet. At the window they fell nets, purfes, laces, &c: Over it is an infcription on a ftone tablet, " *He that giveth to the poor, lendeth to the Lord.*" The act for preferving the health of prifoners, painted on a board, is hung up in the debtors hall.

The men-felons ward on the other fide is down 11

ſteps :

fteps : That adjoining, for women, down 10. There is a new room, level with the ground, 31 feet by 14, with oppofite and lofty windows, for prifoners committed on fufpicion of felony. At the inner door of this prifon, which is of iron grates, I have feen liquors handed to thofe who feemed to have had enough before.—Formerly there was no water in this prifon, but when there was too much; that is, in a very high flood; then it flows into the rooms : Now water is laid in,—Gaoler, a fheriff's officer for city and county.

It were in vain to offer any hints of improvement. This gaol cannot be made a good one.

The corporation pays free-ward debtors 1s. 2d. ¾ a week by a legacy of Mr Peacock. No memorial of this in the gaol. But there is a memorandum of another legacy, viz. of Elizabeth Taylor, who by her will dated 21ft of October 1580, left 3s. 4d. to be divided equally among the prifoners in Oufebridge gaol on Lady-day. This has not been received by them for fome years.

GAOLER's FEES fettled and ORDERS made &c.

	l.	s.	d.
For the difcharge of every debtor for the firft action, to the gaoler	0	5	4
And for the difcharge of every other action to him	0	1	0
To the porter or turnkey for the firft action	0	1	0
And for every other action to him	0	0	6
For the difcharge of every other perfon from the affizes or feffions to the gaoler	0	6	8
And to the turnkey	0	1	0
For the firft week's diet of all perfons in the upper gaol	0	7	0

And for all further time as the prifoner and gaoler can agree.
    And the gaoler is to permit prifoners to provide their own diet after the firft week if the prifoner pleafes

For lodging if the gaoler finds bed bedding and fheets for the firft night	0	0	6

R 2

And

	l.	s.	d.
And for every other night — —	0	0	3
And if two lie in one bed for the first night each	0	0	4
And for the second and every other night each —	0	0	2
For lodging in the upper gaol if the prisoner finds his own bed,			
bedding and sheets for every week —	0	0	6
If two in a bed each — — —	0	0	3

And every prisoner shall have liberty of finding the same if he thinks proper.

And the gaoler shall have liberty if he sees occasion to have two beds in each room and no more.

And it is ordered that every person of what degree or condition soever —who shall use—swearing, cursing, railing or other indecent behaviour—shall—pay for every such offence twelve pence t the gaoler or his deputy on demand ; and on refusal—to be levied by distress on goods—or stopped out of share of box-money—or stand in charge to be paid before release—the fines to be distributed at gaoler's discretion amongst the most needful in the low gaol.

Every prisoner who attempts—or assists an escape—to be ironed.

Those who mutiny on gaoler or deputies—or hinder or disturb &c.— to be kept in close confinement.

On default of weekly payments aforesaid—after demand and refusal— a prisoner may be moved from the master's side—to the common room.

YORK CITY BRIDEWELL

Has a day-room for men, and another for women : The latter is damp. Down 4 steps are five night-rooms for men ; and a large one, with barrack bedsteads for women. The whole dirty and offensive. No court : No water : No sewer. Keeper's salary, 20l. Fees, 2s. Straw, 5l. a year : No bread allowance. At one of my visits some prisoners were employed, in beating or pounding tile-sherds for the bricklayers.

St PETER's GAOL,

For the liberty of St Peter of York, near the Minster gate, is the property of the dean ; who holds his courts
here:

here. He has lately purchafed an adjoining tenement for his gaoler to live in; in confequence, the two rooms in which he lived before are added to the debtors apartments, and they have now four rooms. Under thefe are two cells for criminals. All out of repair: No court: No fewers. No allowance, but a chaldron of coals at Chriftmas.

There is a printed lift of parifhes, towns, and parts of towns which are in the liberty of St Peter. Within the city and ainfty, nine places: In the Faft-Riding, fixity-two; Weft-Riding, forty; North-Riding, fifty-one: And there is one place in each of the following coun ies; Devonfhire, Gloucefterfhire, Lancafhire, Lincolnfhire, Northumberland, Southampton, i. e. Hants. In Nottinghamfhire, feven places.

Gaoler a bailiff: No falary. He pays rent, 4l. Fees, 6s. 8d. No table.

BEVERLEY TOWN GAOL

Has on the ground floor two rooms not fronting the ftreet, for men criminals: And above, a room for women; and two rooms for debtors. No water: No ftraw. Keeper no falary, but as fergeant at mace has 3l. Fees 4s. No table. Licence for beer.

The HALL-GARTH, for Debtors,

In the liberty of St John's of Beverley, the property of Charles Anderfon Pelham, Efq; built a few years fince, has over the hall five fizeable rooms; two of them have fire-places. No court: No water: Fees, 4s. 1d. No table.

table. There is a lift of 113 towns or parts of towns, that are within the liberty of St John's of Beverley or Beverley-Hall-Garth.

R I C H M O N D   G A O L,

For the very extenfive liberty of Richmond and Richmondfhire, the property of Lord Holdernefs, *now* of the Marquis of Carnarvon. It is alfo the bridewell, and the borough gaol. For debtors, a kitchen and bed-room, clofe glazed. For men-criminals, two dungeons down 5 fteps: For women, a room above. No ftraw. Claufes againft fpirituous liquors hung up. A court, and a well. Gaoler a bailiff: No falary for the liberty: For the bridewell, l. 13 : 10 : 0: For the borough, 4l. Pays window-tax: Fees, debtors, 6s. 8d. entrance, and 6s. 8d. at difcharge: Criminals, 16s. 4d: Allowance to the latter, four pence a day.

In the table of fees, dated 1671, and figned *W Wylde* and *Ty Lyttleton*, the 12th article is, " Every perfon or " perfons that fhall be committed upon any warrant—— " upon his or their commitment to gaol fhall pay to the " reft of the prifoners, 2s. 4d. for their *garnifh*."

R I P P O N   L I B E R T Y   G A O L,

Is the property of the Archbifhop, by a charter from king Edward IV. His court adjoining, is called the *Court Military*. The liberty includes twenty-four parifhes. For debtors, four or five good rooms in the keeper's houfe; but no free ward. For felons, one ftrong room quite dark; another with a little window. Formerly there was a deep dungeon, but the prefent fteward, inftead of repairing it, very humanely ordered it to be filled up. Keeper, no falary; he pays rent: He is a bailiff. Fees, debtors, 13s· 4d. No table: Licence for beer·

RIPPON GAOL,

For the Canon-Fee Court, belongs to the dean and chapter of Rippon. It is not only a gaol for that court; but a houfe of correction for the liberty. Two or three rooms for debtors, but no free ward. The bridewell part, two dark rooms, about 8 feet fquare. No court: No water. No falary as gaoler; as keeper of bridewell, l· 10 · 10 · 0. Fees, debtors, 13s. 4d. No table: Licence for beer· Keeper a bailiff.

KNARESBOROUGH PRISON, for DEBTORS,

In the honour or foreft of Knarefborough, the liberty including nineteen townfhips &c. is the property of the duke of Devonfhire, leffee to his Majefty. It is almoft the only remains of a caftle granted by king Edward III. to John of Gaunt duke of Lancafter. One room about 12 feet fquare, is *now* boarded, has a chimney, and the window is glazed: Another inner room is about 8 feet fquare, and has no window. No court: No fewer: No water. Keeper lives diftant: Salary none: Fees, 6s. 8d.

KNARESBOROUGH PRISON, for Town DEBTORS,

Is under the hall. Of difficult accefs; the door about 4 feet from the ground. Only one room, about 12 feet fquare: Window 17 inches by 6. Earth floor: No fireplace: Very offenfive; a common fewer from the town running through it uncovered. I was informed that an officer, confined here fome years fince, for only a few

days,

days, took in with him a dog to defend him from vermin; but the dog was soon deftroyed, and the prifoner's
face much disfigured by them.

KNARESBOROUGH TOWN GAOL.

Is under the landing-place between two flights of ftone
fteps, that lead up to the hall. Only one room about 8
feet by 5: Two windows 18 inches by 6. I mention
this fmall prifon, becaufe in it are fometimes confined
for a night or two at quarter feffions fix or feven prifoners,
men and women.

DONCASTER TOWN GAOL.

Two rooms for felons, and two over them for debtors:
All have chimneys. No water. Keeper one of the fergeants at mace, lives diftant. Fees, 1s. 4d. Allowance
to felons, 4d a day.

BRADFORD PRISON,

For Debtors from the Court of Requefts, for Halifax,
&c. &c.

A new prifon, confifting of four rooms, and a work-
room. Court not fecure: No water. The deputy
keeper pays rent l. 2 : 5 : o for his houfe to the gaoler,
who pays rent to the clerk of the court, by whom he is
appointed. Prifoners are difcharged at the end of three
calendar months. Fees, 5s.

LEEDS TOWN GAOL.

Four good rooms, and a fmall one. No chimney: No
court: No water: No fewer. Keeper lives diftant.
KINGSTON

Kingston upon HULL TOWN and COUNTY GAOL.

The *debtors* ward is a large room. Over it one as large, and over that, another fmaller, both for *criminals*. The ground-room is a damp dungeon: But the gaoler, who has a character for humanity, affured me that no one had been confined in it for many years. In his houfe adjoining is a room or two with beds, for thofe who pay. Leads for debtors to walk on: No court: No water acceffible to criminals: No fewer; and the felons rooms are offenfive. Gaoler no falary: Fees, 13s. 4d. No table. Allowance to felons, three pence a day. Gaol delivery once in three years. The act for preferving the health of prifoners, is hung up.

Kingston upon HULL BRIDEWELL.

Two rooms below, and two up ftairs, about 12 feet fquare; very offenfive: No fire-place. Court only 22 feet by 10; not fecure, and prifoners not permitted to go to the pump: No fewer: No allowance: No ftraw. Not white-wafhed fince it was built. Debtors from the court of confcience fent hither.

The prifoners pound tile-fherds to mix in mortar (for which they have 2d.$\frac{1}{2}$ a bufhel); and pick oakum (for which they are allowed 4d.$\frac{1}{2}$ per ftone). Keeper's falary, 5l. a chaldron of coals; and four thoufand turfs: Fees, 2s. 6d. No table.

SHEFFIELD PRISON, for Debtors.

For the liberty of Hallamfhire, is the property of the duke of Norfolk, now of the earl of Surry. The two

S   lower

lower rooms are free wards: There are two rooms over them. The court is only about 10 feet fquare. Both this and the other prifon might be enlarged on ground ad-jacent that belongs to his lordfhip. Keeper no falary: He rents a public houfe joining to the prifon. Debtors from the court of requefts are difcharged at the end of thirteen weeks.

SHEFFIELD TOWN GAOL.

The *Lobbies* under the town-hall are two fmall rooms, the largeft only about 8 feet fquare, and 6 high. Aper-ture in the door of 6 inches diameter. When the quarter feffions for the Weft-Riding are held at this town, offen-ders are locked up a night or two in this prifon.

ROTHWELL PRISON, for DEBTORS,

Belongs to the liberty of the honour of Pontefract in the duchy court of Lancafter. Is out of repair. A new prifon is lately built at

B A T L E Y.

Behind a houfe for the keeper is the prifon. Plan rect-angular: The front is the wall and gate. On three fides are rooms for men-debtors; five or fix about 10 feet fquare; four much larger for two beds in each. Two day-rooms; two work rooms, and a dark room for the un-ruly. There are in a *feparate court* two rooms for wo-men-debtors: A provifion very kind and prudent, and, I believe, peculiar to this prifon. All the prifon rooms are on the ground floor. The keeper has no falary. Fees, *fee table.*

I

I wifh my reader be not tired with fo many tables of fees, even for the counties. Yet I think I muft not omit the fees which I faw in this private prifon at Rothwell : Becaufe fome of them are high ; and at Halifax they are the fame. The table, at my firft vifit, was regularly figned, 11th Jan. 1732. At my laft vifit at Batley, I found a new table of fees, dated 26th July 1776, the fums entirely the fame.

l. s. d.

Imprimis. That every gentleman fhall pay for his firft week's commons at table, and for his commitment fee   —   0 16 0
And for every week following   —   —   0   5 0
Item. Every yeoman, tradefman, or artificer, for the firft week's commons at table and commitment fee   —   —   0 13 4
And for every week following   —   —   0   4 0
And be it further ordered, that every gentlemen fhall pay nightly for his bed   —   —   —   —   0   0 4
And every yeoman, tradefman, or artificer, lodging in good rooms and on feather beds   0   0 2
And it is alfo ordered that when the gaoler lodgeth two or more prifoners in one bed they fhall pay amongft them *per* night according to their numbers   —   —   0   0 3
And that every prifoner fhall have liberty to provide for him or herfelf whatever neceffaries he or fhe fhall want from any perfon or place whatfoever.
And that every prifoner fhall be furnifhed with neceffaries according to his, her or their degrees and quality, paying a reafonable price for the fame.
And that but one fee fhall be taken by the gaoler for any prifoner's difcharge, although there has been more than one action againft him or her, which fee fhall be   —   —   0 17 4
And to the turnkey   —   —   —   —   0   1 0
Item. For allowing every *fuperfedeas* in every action   —   0   6 8
Item. For allowing every writ of *habeas corpus* befides conduct money to be paid and allowed according to the diftance from the faid gaol to the place where the body is to be removed   0   6 8

H A L I F A X   P R I S O N,

For the manor of Wakefield, dated 1662, is the property of the duke of Leeds. For mafter's-fide debtors, rooms in the keeper's public houfe. Through this you

pafs

pafs to a court about 14 yards by 7 : At the further end of which is a fizeable room on the ground floor for common-fide debtors, it is called the *Low Gaol:* Over it a chamber (the *Low Gaol Chamber*) where prifoners pay one fhilling a week. The whole prifon greatly out of repair : It rained in upon the beds : The rooms were clean. Keeper, no falary : He pays the duke 24l. a year : Fees, fee Batley, preceding page.

COUNTY GAOL AT DURHAM.

GAOLER,	*Bainbridge Watfon,* now *Thomas Bungey,* by patent from the bifhop *durante bene placito.*	
Salary,	None.	
Fees,	Debtors, —	l. o - 10 - o.
	Felons at Affize, —	o - 16 - 8.
	———at Quarter Seffions,	o - 13 - 4.
Tranfports,	about l. 10 - 10 - o each.	
Licence,	Beer and Wine.	
PRISONERS,		
Allowance,	Debtors, none.	
	Felons, two pence a day.	
Garnifh,	Debtors, l. o - 4 - 6.	
	Felons, o - 1 - o.	
CHAPLAIN,	Rev. Mr *Decent.*	
Duty,	Sunday and Thurfday.	
Salary,	40l.	
SURGEON,	Mr *Bainbridge.*	
Salary,	None ; He makes a bill.	

THE high gaol is the property of the bifhop. By patent from his Lordfhip, Sir Hedworth Williamfon, Bart. is perpetual fheriff. The court for mafter's-fide debtors is only 24 feet by 10. Common-fide debtors have none at all : Their free wards, the *Low Gaol,* are two damp unhealthy rooms 10 feet 4 inches fquare, by the gate-way : They are never fuffered to go out of thefe unlefs to chapel,
which

which is the mafter's-fide debtors hall ; and not always to
that : For on a S*nday when I was there and miffed them
at chapel, they told me they were not permitted to go
thither.   No fewers : At more than one of my vifits, I
learned that the dirt, afhes, &c. had lain there many
months.   There is an excellent double-barreled pump,
which raifes water above 70 feet.

Felons have no court ; but they have a day-room and
two fmall rooms for an infirmary.   The men are put at
night into dungeons : One 7 feet fquare for three prifoners : Another, the *Great Hole*, 17 feet by 12, has only a
little window.   In this I faw fix prifoners, (in 1776) moft
of them *tranfports*, chained to the floor.   In that fituation
they had been many weeks ; and were very fickly.   Their
ftraw on the ftone floor almoft worn to duft.   Long confinement, and not having the king's allowance of 2s. 6d. a
week, had urged them to attempt an *efcape :* after which
the gaoler chained them as above.   There is another
dungeon for women-felons 12 feet by 8 ; and up ftairs a
feparate room or two.

The common-fide debtors in the *low gaol*, whom I faw
eating boiled bread and water, told me, that this was the
only nourifhment fome had lived upon for near a twelve-
month.   They have from a legacy one fhilling and fixpence a week in winter, and one fhilling a week in fummer for coals.   No memorandum of it in the gaol ; perhaps this may in time be loft, as the gaoler faid two others
'were, *viz.* one of bifhop Crewe, and another of bifhop
Wood ; from which prifoners had received no benefit for
fome years paft.   But now the bifhop has humanely filed
bills in chancery for the recovery of thefe legacies.   The
claufes againft fpirituous liquors are hung up.   Gaol delivery *once* a year.   At my laft vifit there were five boys between

tween thirteen and fifteen years of age, confined with the moſt profligate and abandoned.

There was a vacant piece of ground adjacent, of little uſe but for the gaoler's occaſional lumber. It extends to the river, and meaſures about 22 yards by 16. I once and again adviſed the encloſing this for a court: But when I was there in January 1776, I had the mortification to hear that the ſurgeon, who was uncle to the gaoler, had obtained from the biſhop in October preceding, a leaſe of it for twenty-one years, at the rent of one ſhilling *per annum.* He had built a little ſtable on it.

TABLE of FEES, &c.

RULES and ORDERS eſtabliſhed by the—Juſtices for the County Palatinate of Durham and Sadberge at their General Quarter Seſſions—16th July 1729—and Fees allowed to be taken by the Keeper of the ſaid Gaol and his Officers as follows:

	l.	s.	d.
Imprimis, For every priſoner lodging in either of the common-ſides commonly called the low gaol, no chamber-rent			
Item For an entire chamber without a bed-fellow in the high gaol	0	3	6
For lodging with a bed-fellow in any other chamber except the common chamber, for each priſoner every week —	0	2	0
For lodging with a bed-fellow in the common chamber, of each priſoner every week — — — —	0	1	3
For lodging in a ſingle bed in that common chamber without admitting of a bed-fellow in every week — —	0	2	6
Out of which abatement ſhall be made			
For every priſoner that findeth his own bedding bedclothes and ſheets and admitting a bed-fellow with him every week	0	0	4

For Diet of Priſoners.

	l.	s.	d.
Item For every knight for every week — —	0	10	0
Of every eſquire or gentleman not exceeding for every week	0	7	6
Item Of every yeoman artificer or labourer not exceeding weekly	0	6	0
For wine ale and brandy at the common rates uſed in the town.			

For Liberates or Final Diſcharges of Priſoners.

	l.	s.	d.
Item For the diſcharge of every priſoner upon proceſs or order from the court of chancery — —	0	10	0

For

	l.	s.	d.
For the firſt liberate — — —	0	1	0
Item For every knight eſquire or gentleman for the ſecond ditto	0	3	9
For every one more — — —	0	1	6
Item For every yeoman artificer or labourer for the firſt	0	8	8
For the ſecond — — —	0	3	9
For every one more — — —	0	1	6

Fees to the Under Keeper and Door Keeper.

	l.	s.	d.
Item For attendance of every priſoner that goeth abroad into the town every time — — —	0	0	4
For every knight eſquire or gentleman for his final diſcharge and enlargement only — — —	0	0	6
For every yeoman artificer or labourer for ſuch diſcharge	0	0	0

COUNTY BRIDEWELL at DURHAM,

Was built, as appears by the date over the door, in 1634. Being on the ſide of a hill, the rooms are airy. No court: No water: The late keeper Watſon had a garden which he let for a guinea a year. He lived at the high gaol; and put in a woman to take care of this priſon. But the juſtices have now very properly put in a keeper who reſides in the priſon; at my laſt viſit the houſe was clean, the priſoners were at work, and their looks beſpoke the attention of a good keeper. Salary, 30l. and ten guineas from the rents of the adjoining houſes.

NEWCASTLE TOWN and COUNTY GAOL.

GAOLER,	John Craſter, now Thomas Harle.
Salary,	50l. and 2l. gown-money.
Fees,	Debtors, l. 0 - 10 - 8.
	Felons, 0 - 14 - 4.
Tranſports,	Only expence.
Licence,	Now Beer and Wine.

PRISONERS,

Allowance,	Debtors, two pence a day, on petition.
	Felons, two pence a day.
Garniſh,	Lately cancelled.

CHAPLAINS,

CHAPLAINS, Rev. Mr *Brunton*, and Rev. Mr *Brand*.
Duty,   On Sunday none ; but on two other days prayers :
              And once a month fermon.   None of the days fixed.
              The chaplains officiate alternately a month each.
Salary,   10l. the corporation, and 10l. Sir W. Blacket.
SURGEON,   Mr *Bacon*, now Mr *Maxfield*.
Salary,   None : He makes a bill.

In this Newgate, which is the gate at the upper end of
the town, all the rooms except the condemned room are
up ftairs, and airy : I always found them remarkably
clean, ftrewed with fand, &c.   The corporation allow
both debtors and felons firing and candles in plenty : And
every prifoner has a chaff bed, two blankets, and a coverlet : Debtors and felons are not thus accommodated in
any other prifon in England.   They alfo allow brooms,
mops, and all fuch neceffaries.   The fums generoufly allowed for thofe articles, amount to l. 45 : 1 : 4 *per annum*.
This is one of the very few gaols that have what is called in
London the *rules*.   Part of two ftreets near the gaol is in
the prifon-liberty.

The debtors walk on the battery at the top of the gaol,
which is 38 feet by 34.   There is no court : But one
might be made of the vacant ground that lies weft of the
gaol.   The debtors beds are in clofets : If on iron bedfteads and in the wards (as in fome hofpitals) it would be
more falutary.   No prifoners here have fetters, unlefs
they be riotous.   For fome years paft, prifoners acquitted have been difcharged in court ; the corporation paid
the gaoler's fees if the prifoners were poor.—Gaol delivery *once* a year.

I was concerned to find that the humane gaoler Crafter
was dead.   But his fucceffor Mr Harle is equally worthy
of the truft.

                                                        Dr

Dr Rotheram, a phyfician in this town, vifits the prifoners very affiduoufly without fee or reward. This is the
only inftance of the kind I have met with.

The act for preferving the health of prifoners was hung
up, both on the debtors and felons fide. Claufes againft
fpirituous liquors not hung up.

A palifaded wall is erected at a little diftance from the
felons window, to prevent flies, &c. being conveyed to
them.

An exact Copy of the RATES and FEES to be from henceforth received by
—the Gaoler or Keeper of his Majefty's Gaol—called Newgate within
this town of Newcaftle upon Tyne—fettled—at the General Quarter Seffions held at Guildhall in Newcaftle aforefaid, on the 15th of July Anno
Domini 1730. And approved of at the Affize following hy Francis Page
and John Fortefcue A two of his faid Majefty's Judges of Affize According to an Act of Parliament lately made

	l.	s.	d.
Every prifoner upon any civil action fhall pay to the keeper at his firft coming in	0	3	0
Every prifoner charged by procefs or procefſes out of the court of record held before the mayor and fheriff of the faid town of Newcaftle upon Tyne refpectively fhall pay to the faid keeper upon his difcharge from the faid procefs or procefſes only	0	6	8
Every prifoner charged upon any execution or executions out of the court of confcience held within the faid town fhall pay to the faid keeper upon his difcharge from the faid execution or executions	0	2	0
Every prifoner on any criminal account or accounts whatfoever fhall pay unto the faid keeper upon his difcharge only	0	13	4
Every perfon appearing upon a recognizance at the affizes and after-wards tried upon an indictment or indictments whatfoever and fhall be committed thereon fhall pay to the faid keeper upon his difcharge	0	6	8
Every prifoner fhall pay to the turnkey of the faid gaol or prifon upon his difcharge	0	1	0

There are alfo at NEWCASTLE,

A BRIDEWELL. A room for men; another for women. A new building is now added, confifting of fix
T rooms.

rooms. Three of them on the ground floor, are 17 feet by 12, and arched with brick. The walls of the court not being secure, the prisoners have no access to it. Their allowance is two pence a day, and firing. The keeper is a sergeant at mace. He has no salary, but the profit of the prisoners work. The water is lately brought *near* the prison.*

A small GAOL, the *Tower of the Close*, consisting of three rooms over the gate-way. No court: No water. Allowance two pence a day.

COUNTY GAOL AT MORPETH.

GAOLER, *John Kent.*
    Salary, None.
    Fees, Debtors, l. 0 - 12 - 6.
            Felons, 1 - 3 - 0.
    Transports, Only expences.
    Licence, Beer.

PRISONERS,
    Allowance, Debtors, none but on applying to justices.
            Felons, two pence a day each, paid *once a month.*
    Garnish, l. 0 - 1 - 4.

CHAPLAIN, Rev. Mr *Nicholfon.*
    Duty, Sunday, Tuesday, Friday.
    Salary, 10l. and 5l. for condemned felons; lately raised to 30l.

SURGEON, Mr *Laidman.*
    Salary, None: He makes a bill.

THE debtors have six sizeable rooms which are out of repair. Some commodious rooms lately built are occupied by the gaoler. Only one court, which is for debtors.

                                Felons

---

* Where prisoners are always locked up, there should be water laid into each ward, as I have seen in foreign houses of correction.

Felons are always locked in the *tower.* In the women's room I faw (Jan. 1776) two; who, the gaoler faid, were caft for tranfportation; one in Sept. 1773, the other in Nov. 1774: But at my laft vifit, I found they had been humanely releafed at the affize.

Of the other two rooms, generally appropriated to men-felons, one is a day-room, the other an offenfive dungeon, the window only 18 inches by 9. In the latter were three tranfports (1776) who, upon *fufpicion* of *intending* an efcape, were chained to the floor. They had not the king's allowance of 2s. 6d. a week.

Gaol delivery *once* a year. Affize held at Newcaftle, whither prifoners are conveyed; and men and women confined together four or five nights in a dirty damp dungeon down 6 fteps in the old caftle, which having no roof, in a wet feafon the water is fome inches deep.

The county has for fome years paid the gaoler's fees for acquitted prifoners, if poor: And clothed fuch tranfports as were quite indigent.

The debtors court fhould be allotted to felons: And one for debtors might be taken from the gaoler's fpacious garden.

Claufes againft fpirituous liquors are hung up. The act for preferving the health of prifoners, painted on a board, was in the debtors hall or chapel. The following table of fees is framed and glazed.

TABLE of FEES &c. Settled and allowed to be due to the Keeper of his Majefty's Gaol at Morpeth—by the Juftices—at the Quarter Seffions--- held——at Hexham 1759.

Commit-

Commitment Fees.

Every debtor l. o - 1 - 4   Every felon l. o - 2 - 8.

Chamber-Rents.

	l.	*s.*	*d.*
To the room called the green room with one bed in it and if only one perfon will have it to himfelf, to pay weekly ——	o	2	6
If two perfons therein to pay each —— ——	o	1	6
To the room called Burton's room having two beds. and the gaoler finding bedding and linen, each perfon to pay weekly	o	1	o
But if one will have a bed is to pay —— ——	o	2	o
To the little green room having one bed and if one perfon will have it to himfelf he is to pay weekly ——	o	2	6
If two therein only to pay each — —	o	1	6
The gaoler finding good and wholefome bedding To the room called the fencing room with three beds and the gaoler finding wholefome linen each perfon to pay weekly	o	1	o
To the little room called Mrs Carr's room the gaoler finding beds and linen each perfon is to pay weekly — —	o	1	o
If the prifoner finds the bedding — —	o	o	6
To a room called Mr Johnfon's room ; being on the fame floor, the gaoler finding bed and linen each perfon to pay	o	1	o
If they find their own bedding, only — —	o	o	6
There is a large room that prifoners pay nothing for, which holds a great many beds, called the middle tower			
Every debtor upon his difcharge to pay to the gaoler ——	o	10	2
To the turnkey — — —	o	1	o
Every felon on his difcharge — — —	o	18	4
To the turnkey — — —	o	2	o

COUNTY BRIDEWELL at MORPETH.

The three lower rooms are clofe. That above for women is larger and more airy. The court not being fecure, the prifoners are generally locked up. Over the way is a long room (72 feet) which is a warehoufe and work-fhop: And above it another work-fhop. The keeper, a clothier, employs his prifoners; the men and boys from eight o'clock to four, at two fhillings a week: Women from eight to five, at one fhilling and fixpence a week. He gives them alfo firing. No county allowance. His falary, 3ol. No fees.

BERWICK

BERWICK * TOWN and COUNTY GAOL.

GAOLER, *John Richardfon.*
   Salary, 16l.

  Fees, Debtors, Freemen, Felons, } none.

Debtors not free, l. 0 - 2 - 6.
  Licence, Beer.

PRISONERS,
  Allowance, Debtors, Freemen, four pence a day, and coals.

Ditto, not free, Felons, } two pence halfpenny a day.

  Garnish, l. 0 : 1 : 0.

CHAPLAIN, None.

SURGEON, None; but on application to the magistrates.

This gaol is part of the grand town-hall, which was built in 1757, and has a fine steeple: The only one in the town. The four rooms or cells on the ground floor are damp, and prisoners are not put into them, but over the hall, where is a large room, or gallery, and seven other rooms, sizeable, but dirty. No court: No water. Clauses against spirituous liquors not hung up. The gaoler keeps a public house. He told me he went to the gaol thrice a day; at nine, one, and eight.

COUNTY GAOL at CARLISLE.

GAOLER, *Brathwaite Atkinfon,* now *Thomas Dixon.*
   Salary, 21l.

                                             Fees,

* This place, though a distinct jurisdiction, in none of the circuits, is inferted here, rather than at the end of the English and Welfh counties, because its situation gives it a natural connection with the last-mentioned county, and it falls in here in the order of my journey through the northern part of the kingdom.

Fees, Debtors, } l. 0 - 11 - 0.
    Felons, }

Tranfports, 1l. each to Whitehaven.
Licence, Beer. The tap let.

PRISONERS,
 Allowance, Debtors, on applying to the juftices fome obtain a fhil-
     ling a week, fome nine pence.
    Felons, nine pence a week *before* conviction; a fhil-
     ling *after*.
 Garnifh, l. 0 - 1 - 0.

CHAPLAIN, Rev. Mr *Farifh*.
 Duty, Sunday, Wednefday, Friday; firft Sunday in the
    month, fermon.
 Salary, 20l.

SURGEON, Mr *Lofh*.
 Salary, l. 2 - 2 - 0 for attendance. Medicines paid for by
    bill.

THE court fpacious, 85 yards by 36: It was common
to all prifoners; but now a part is appropriated to the felons, and feparated by iron palifades. In the court is a
chapel, built as appears by the date, in 1734. Five
rooms for mafter's-fide debtors; and as many on the common-fide. Moft of the latter are large, but have windows
to the ftreet. Where there are fo many rooms, not to
feparate the men and women is certainly inexcufable.

The wards for felons are two rooms down a ftep or
two; dark and dirty. One of them, the day-room, had
a window to the ftreet; through which fpirituous liquors
and tools for mifchief might be eafily conveyed: But it is
now bricked up. The night-room is only 11 feet by 9:
At my laft vifit, *men* and *women* were lodged together in
it. Two rooms over the felons wards, which have been
ufed as tap-rooms, feem to be intended for the *women*
only, but in *one* of thefe I alfo found *three men* and *four women* lodged together. No infirmary. Tranfports had
               not

not the king's allowance of 2s. 6d. a week. Claufes againft fpirituous liquors, and act for preferving the health of prifoners, not hung up. Gaol delivery *once* a year. Few gaols have fo many convenient rooms for common-fide debtors. It is the more remarkable here, becaufe there is *no table* figned by the magiftrates to particularize the free wards. Some gaolers avail themfelves of fuch a circumftance, and demand rent for rooms which were undoubtedly defigned for common-fide prifoners.

The gaol fever, which fome years ago carried off many of the prifoners, did not deter Mr Farifh from vifiting the fick every day.

COUNTY BRIDEWELL at COCKERMOUTH,

Is behind the keeper's houfe, and part of it his free-hold. A room on the ground floor, the *Strong Room.* Up ftairs another room; and a clofet called the *Lunatic Room.* All out of repair, and infecure: And fo is the court, which I fuppofe is the reafon that many for fmall offences are fent to the county gaol. No allowance: No ftraw. Keeper's falary or rent, 20l. No fees.

CARLISLE CITY GAOL,

Over the Scotch-gate. Only one ruinous room about 20 feet fquare; with a window 4 feet by 1½ No allow-ance, but a very fmall quantity of peat taken as a toll upon that commodity, and water brought twice a day.

I was told that many a poor traveller from the north, who by fome calamity had contracted an unavoidable debt of forty fhillings, has been confined at a diftance from his

friends

friends in this prifon, where there is no provifion, ncr any means of procuring it.

WHITEHAVEN TOWN GAOL.

Is part of the work-houfe· Two rooms up-ftairs; and a dungeon in which they ufed to confine tranfports brought hither to be fhipped. All dirty and offenfive.

WESTMORLAND.

COUNTY GAOL AT APPLEBY.

GAOLER, *Benjamin Ainfley.*
 Salary, rol.
 Fees, Debtors, ⎱ l. o - 6 - 8.
     Felons, ⎰
 Tranfports, a fhilling a mile each to Whitehaven.
 Licence, Beer.
PRISONERS,
 Allowance, Debtors, none.
     Felons, four pence a day each.
 Garnifh, l. o - 1 - o.
CHAPLAIN, None.
SURGEON, None.

APPLEBY.

THIS gaol was built by the county. The earl of Thanet is hereditary fheriff, and pays the gaoler his falary· Happily for the prifoners in a gaol fo circumftanced, the prefent gaoler is a man of temper and humanity.

I formerly complained of this prifon being within reach of floods: But in Jan. 1776, there was a new building on the higheſt part of the yard. It conſiſts of four vaulted wards for felons, 15 feet by 13; a window in each, but no chimney: And over them three good rooms with chimneys; for debtors.

Gaol delivery *once* a year.——No table of fees. The act for preſerving the health of priſoners not hung up.

COUNTY BRIDEWELLS.

A P P L E B Y.

Two rooms, 11½ feet by 8½: No chimney: Each has a ſmall window into a ſtable: Subject to floods.——No allowance. Keeper's ſalary, 8l. No fees.

K E N D A L.

Only one room for men and women, 18 feet by 13, with one window about two feet ſquare: No chim ney: No court: No water: No ſewer. The keeper has a garden: Salary, l. 6 - 10 - 0. No fees.——The town fometimes commits priſoners hither, and allows them ſix pence a day; the county four pence.

K E N D A L   T O W N   G A O L.

Only two dungeons under the chapel, called *black holes:* 14 ſteps under ground. No court: No water: No ſtraw. Allowance, ſix pence a day. The two town ſergeants keep the priſon by turns; a week each.

U
LAN-

LANCASHIRE.

COUNTY GAOL, LANCASTER CASTLE.

GAOLER,   *John Dane (since dead).*
   Salary,   None.
   Fees,   Debtors, l. o : 8 : o.
            Felons,   o : 13 : 4.
   Transports, 5l. each.
   Licence,   Beer and Wine.

PRISONERS,
   Allowance,   Debtors, ⎱ one shilling each on Saturday morning.
              Felons, ⎰
   Garnish,   Debtors, l. o - 7 - 2.
             Felons,   o - 2 - 6.

CHAPLAIN, Rev. Mr *Spicer,* now Rev. Mr *Watson.*
   Duty,   Sunday twice; Wednesday and Friday once.
   Salary,   50l.

SURGEON,   Mr *Dixon*
   Salary,   Now l. 10 : 10 o.

LANCASTER CASTLE.

THE castle-yard is pacious. Master's-side debtors have many apartments. One of them which they call the *Oven,* is said to have been used as such in the time of John of Gaunt duke of Lancaster: The diameter, 24 feet; the height, that of an ordinary room. The free ward for debtors is large but dark. These, as well as those of the master's-side, are allowed to walk and work (spin, knit, &c.) in the crown and shire halls. The latter is used as a chapel.

Petty offenders are sometimes sent hither, because the bridewells are distant. There is a large room for them near the gate; and they are separate from felons.

Men

Men and women-felons have their day-rooms apart, at the upper end of the court. Women sleep in their day-room. Men have for their night-rooms two vaulted cells. One of them, the *Low Dungeon*, is 10 steps under ground, 21 feet by 9, extremely close, dark, and unwholesome; very hot even in winter. Their other cell, the *High Dungeon*, is larger, but close and offensive, though not under ground.

I once saw three felons sick : The recorder, Mr Fenton, gave immediate orders for their relief by better nourishment, &c. and they soon recovered. No infirmary. Transports had not the king's allowance of 2s. 6d. a week. When prisoners are convicted at Preston or Manchester, and from thence brought hither, the gaoler has a shilling a mile conduct-money for each.

Part of the castle-yard is an inclosed bowling-green.

One of the rooms for debtors (60 feet by 27) is called the *Quaker's Room ;* because, it is said, when those people were so cruelly persecuted in the last century, vast numbers of them were confined in it.

If the large stable which is not much used, and the great room under the shire-hall (in which I saw only one poor lunatic ; who had been there many years, and is since dead) were converted into night-rooms for felons, one small room for each ; and an infirmary were built, this would be a good gaol. From Mr Fenton's humanity, and the regard that is justly paid him, I cannot but hope for some of these improvements.

These remarks were made in 1776 : At my last visit in 1779, I had the pleasure to find six cells made in the old

U 2   stable

ftable, 10 feet 2 inches by 6 feet 8 inches, each having an aperture about 2 feet by 1½; and two good rooms fitted up for an infirmary in one of the towers. The debtors rooms were white-wafhed, and cafements put in their windows: The caftle-yard lowered and paved, which being on a defcent, may eafily be kept clean. The act for preferving the health of prifoners, and the claufes againft fpirituous liquors, hung up very confpicuoufly.

The chaplain's falary, 50l. is from the county, and from the dutchy 4l.

Fees taken by the Gaoler of Lancafter Caftle.

	l.	*s.*	*d.*
For every debtor's difcharge when bv a *fuperfedeas* —	0	8	0
On a common difcharge 8s. and 2s & 6d. for the fheriff's certificate	0	10	6
When a debtor is furrendered in difcharge of his bail	0	2	4
When a debtor is charged with a declaration 2s. & 4d. with the rule to take the prifoner to the bar and 2s. & 4d. with the *remandato* — — —	0	4	8
When a debtor takes the benefit of the infolvent act 1s. and 2s. & 4d. to bring the prifoner to the bar by rule and 2s. & 4d. for the fheriff's certificate. — — —	0	5	8
Fees for all crown prifoners — — —	0	18	0
Lately altered to — — —	0	13	4

M A N C H E S T E R.

Rebuilt as *per* date, in the year 1774. Separate courts and apartments for men and women. Two rooms for an infirmary. The men have work-rooms, over which are chambers. Their 4 night-rooms or cells in a paffage or long room 45 feet by 6, are clofe; 11 feet by 8; 11 fteps below the court; but not properly under ground, being on the declivity of a hill. Women have three rooms on the ground floor, and three chambers: Here is a dungeon, down 9 fteps, 14 feet by 13; but women are not put there. The iron-grate door into each court has faft-

enings

enings of a contrivance fingularly curious. No allowance, Keeper's falary lately raifed from 25l. to 60, in lieu of fees.

At my laft vifit the act for preferving the health of prifoners. and the claufes againft fpirituous liquors, hung up. The keeper is a chandler, and employs the prifoners in fpinning candle-wick at three-halfpence a pound. In the front of the prifon is a ftone with an aperture into a box, having this infcription ;—" *Sick, and in prifon, and ye vifited me not.*" Matt. xxv. 43.

LIVERPOOL * BOROUGH GAOL,

Out of repair. Apartments clofe and dirty. Seven clofe dungeons 10 fteps under ground ; each 6½ feet by 5 feet 9 inches, and 6 feet high. Three prifoners are locked up in each of them at night. There is another dungeon, larger, but not fecure. No infirmary. The keeper told me in Nov. 1775, that after I was there laft year and faid his prifoners were in danger of the gaol fever, twenty-eight of them had been ill of it at one time. What led me to think fo was, the offenfivenefs of the dungeons, and the number of prifoners. The prifon is furrounded with other buildings, and cannot be made healthy and convenient. Allowance in common on Sunday, bread 4s. beef and broth about 6s. Firing from October to May. Gaoler, Rofendale Allen, ferjeant at mace, paid the widow of the late gaoler, 20l. a year ; and put in a deputy who paid him 65l. a year. Fees, debtors, felons, &c. 4s. 6d. No table. Chaplain, duty, —Tuefday

---

* The Gentlemen of this Corporation will pleafe to accept my grateful acknowledgments for the honour done me in prefenting me with the freedom of the town.

—Tuefday and Friday : Salary, l. 12 : 12 : 0.—Claufes againft fpirituous liquors not hung up.

Felons are generally fent to Lancafter caftle : The prifoners kept here are for the moft part debtors.

At my vifit in 1779, this gaol was much cleaner than at my former vifits : The court paved : The act for preferving the health of prifoners hung up ; but the unhealthy dungeons ftill in ufe. The furgeon, Mr Shertcliffe, whofe falary is 10l. informed me, that many more had the gaol fever in 1775, than I mentioned in my publication. The gaoler now is Mr Thomas Lyon : His falary, 10l.

LIVERPOOL BRIDEWELL.

This prifon was built in 1776, on an eminence adjoining the work-houfe, near the town. The men and women have feparate rooms, courts, &c. The women have fix rooms below, and the fame number above : The men have four rooms below and four above. Thefe are twelve feet by 10 ; are furnifhed with bedfteads ; but are too clofe, having no window, only an aperture in the door about 9 inches fquare, and another near the ceiling. They have a large *work-room*, in which was only one boy. Near this room in the men's court is a *pump*, to which the women are tied *every week* and receive difcipline. In this court is alfo a *bath*, with a new and fingular contrivance. At one end of it is a ftandard for a long pole, at the extremity of which is faftened a chair. In this all the *females* (not the *males*) at their entrance, after a few queftions, are placed, with a flannel fhift on, and undergo a thorough ducking, thrice repeated—an ufe of a bath, which I dare fay the legiflature never thought of, when in
their

their late act they ordered baths with a view to *cleanliness* and *preserving the health* of prisoners; not for the exercise of a *wanton* and *dangerous* kind of *severity*. The women were employed in picking oakum. Allowance, twopennyworth of bread a day. Keeper's salary, 30l, Matron, 10l.

WARRINGTON TOWN BRIDEWELL.

Two rooms in the work-house yard; one about 9 feet square, with bedstead and straw; the other about 9 feet by 5: No windows. Allowance for diet, the same as the poor, who, by their appearance, seem to have a humane attention paid to them. Keeper, no salary for the bridewell: No fees: Is master of the work-house.

COUNTY GAOL, CHESTER CASTLE.

This castle is the property of the King. The first room is a hall or chapel: There are two staircases leading up from it to four rooms for master's-side debtors. Down 18 steps is a small court, which was common to debtors and felons. It is lately divided, but the high close pales which separate the two courts, now so very small, deprive both debtors and felons of the benefit of fresh air. The former, in their free ward, the *Pope's Kitchen;* the latter, in their day-room, the *king's kitchen.* Both these are 6 steps below the court: Each of them above 35 feet by 22. Near the former is the condemned room· Under the king's kitchen is the *king's cellar;* quite useless. Under the pope's kitchen is a dark room or passage 24 feet by 9: The descent to it, is by 21 steps from the court. No window: Not a breath of fresh air: Only two apertures with grates in the ceiling into the *pope's kitchen* above.

above. On one fide of it are fix cells *(ftalls)* each about 8 feet by 3, with a barrack bedftead, and an aperture over the door about 8 inches by four. In each of thefe are locked up at night, fometimes two or three felons· They pitch thefe dungeons three or four times a year: when I was in one of them, I ordered the door to be fhut; and my fituation brought to mind what I had heard of the *black-hole* at Calcutta.

The felons day-room is not fecure. They efcaped in 1775, by breaking through the flight floor into the king's cellar below; and through the decayed walls of that they made their way down the hill. The keeper, who is careful and humane, was not blameable.

CHESTER CITY and COUNTY GAOL:

This gaol, called the *North gate Prifon*, has many convenient apartments for debtors. The felons day-room is fpacious: But to their dungeon, or night-room (which is 14 feet by 8) the defcent is *now* by 18 fteps: For at my laft vifit, I found that the room was very injudicioufly, (not to fay cruelly) funk fome feet. In it is a barrack bedftead. No light, nor any communication with the external air, but by two leaden pipes of about an inch diameter laid in from the gate-way. The prifoners in March 1774, complained of exceffive heat. The women-felons lie up ftairs, in a room called *the Upper Dungeon*, which has no window, only an aperture in the door (14 inches by 7) into one of the debtors rooms. No bedding or ftraw. The court is common to debtors and felons: But the former have the privilege of walking in the keeper's garden.

COUNTY

COUNTY GAOL AT FLINT.

THIS gaol is alfo a bridewell. On the ground floor are the gaoler's apartments. For debtors there are, up ftairs, a common ward; and two other rooms. They have alfo a court, backwards. For felons and petty of-fenders, two dark clofets, the black holes, on the fame floor as the debtors rooms : They are each 5 feet by 4; and were the only receptacles for criminals till a few years ago, when a dungeon in the yard was added, which is 16 feet by 11. This is down 8 fteps. A court before it about 5 yards fquare: Water laid in. When men are here, women are put in the dark clofets. The claufes againft fpirituous liquors are hung up. The debtors and felons of late not being fatisfied with the kind allowance from the county of 1s. 6d. in bread and 6d. in money per week, the juftices very properly ordered, for the prefent, only a pound of bread a day to each.

Great feffions at Mold: Conveyance thither at the gaoler's expence. He has a falary of 25l. as keeper of the bridewell.

About twenty years ago, here was a debtor who infift-ed upon not being fubject to the gaoler, nor to any orders but fuch as fhould be enjoined by the magiftrates. Upon this occafion, as I was informed, the juftices at the quarter feffions held at Holywell in July 1759, made fome falutary rules for the government of this prifon, which are hung up in the gaol.

COUNTY GAOL AT RUTHIN.

THE old gaol was alfo a county bridewell. A new gaol is almoft finifhed. The front is for the gaoler. Back-

X   wards,

wards, on the ground floor, a day-room or kitchen for debtors 27 feet by 15; and another as large for criminals : and for the latter, four cells $7\frac{1}{2}$ feet by $6\frac{1}{2}$; two on each fide of a paffage only 3 feet wide. The cells are arched with brick, and lined with oak planks. A window in each 3 feet by 1, which was glazed ; but being found too clofe, is now open. In both the debtors and felons day-rooms are 8 cupboards with feparate locks and keys, that each may fecure his provifion. Above, are nine rooms for debtors, and a neat chapel. In each of the debtors rooms is an *iron bedftead*, two chairs, a table, and a fender. Separate courts for debtors and criminals ; in each a pump, and a bathing-room, with a copper, &c.

Gentlemen fo confiderate, will fcarcely forget an infirmary, and feparating women from men, as this is ftill a county bridewell. If a door-way was made between the windows of the felons day-room into their court, they might be more feparated from the debtors.

Great feffions of late, at Wrexham ; and conveyance thither at the gaoler's expence. He has a falary of 20l. as keeper of bridewell. The claufes againft fpirituous liquors are hung up.

AN

A N

A C C O U N T

OF THE PRINCIPAL

LAZARETTOS

I N

Europe, &c.

THE firſt Lazaretto I viſited at MARSEILLES. The Health-office, *Le Bureau de Sante*, is in the city at the end of the port. It has an outer room and two council chambers. In the outer room, the depoſitions of captains of ſhips are taken, who come in their boats to an iron grate. At two feet diſtance there is an iron lattice with a door, which is opened only by the ſervants of the intendants, or directors, who are here in waiting, in a blue livery trimmed with white lace. Here alſo letters, or orders for ſupplies, from the captains who are performing quarantine in their ſhips, are received with a pair of iron tongs, and dipped in a bucket of vinegar ſtanding ready for that purpoſe. Over the book in which the depoſitions of the captains are inſerted for pub-

lic

lic view, their is hung up an advertifement, to defire that
the leaves may not be torn, and if they be torn, that information may be given to the office. In this room are hung
up alfo orders, that when captains are examined, none
but thofe who belong to the office fhall be prefent; and
that captains of merchant-fhips, who have no bills of
health, fhall be obliged themfelves to perform quarantine
in the Lazaretto.

In the firft of the two council chambers, there were
hung up a *plan of the Lazaretto*, and a picture of a perfon
dying of the plague ; alfo the names of the directors, and
the weeks of their attendance. Two or more of them are
prefent every day to take the depofitions of the captains as
they arrive, to fix the guards and porters, and for the
other bufinefs of this extenfive Lazaretto.

The *Lazaretto* is on an elevated rock near the city, at
the end of the bay, fronting the fouth-weft, and com-
mands the entrance of the harbour. It is very fpacious,
and its fituation renders it very commodious for the great
trade which the French carry on in the Levant. Among
other apartments for paffengers, there are 24 large rooms,
of which fome are above ftairs, and open into a fpacious
gallery enclofed by lattice. In thefe rooms are clofets
for beds, which the paffengers and guards are required to
bring with them. The guards are fent by the Health-office, and their number is regulated by the number of paffengers of each fhip who perform quarantine. A number of paffengers not exceeding three, are allowed one
guard, the expence of whom (namely 20 *fous per* day and
his victuals) they are obliged to bear. A paffenger, therefore, who has no companion, has no affiftance in bearing
this expence. To four, five, or fix paffengers, two
guards are affigned ; and to feven three guards. Thefe
                                                guards

guards perform the offices of servants ; and will cook for passengers if they do not choose to have their victuals from the tavern.

Within the Lazaretto is the governor's house ; and a chapel in which divine service is regularly performed ; as also a tavern, from which persons under quarantine may have their dinners and suppers sent them, and which has likewise the exclusive privilege of supplying them with wine. Two days before the quarantine is finished, the bills are sent in, which being paid to the cashier, they receive a clean patent. *

The quarantine of passengers who come with a foul bill, or in one of the two first ships from the same place with a clean bill, is 21 days, including the day they go out. If any account arrive of the plague having broke out in the place from which they come with a clean bill, after they left it, they are allowed no advantage from their clean bill; for, in this case they must be confined 15 days, and also fumigated † before they come down stairs, and are permitted to go to the *parloirs*. In case any of the company to which they belong die, their quarantine recommences.

The *parloirs* are long galleries with seats in them situated

---

* If bills are overcharged, there are magistrates in the city who should examine and tax them : But these magistrates do not always discharge their duty. The chaplain of the Dutch consul at *Smyrna* applied to them as many others have done, without obtaining redress.

† The fumigation is three times repeated, at the expence of nine *livres*, and by many is thought unnecessary. It was not used in the Lazarettos at *Venice*.

ed between the gates, and feparated by wooden baluftrades and wire lattice, beyond which there are other
baluftrades, diftant about 10 feet, at which the perfons
in quarantine may fee and converfe with fuch friends as
may choofe to vifit them. The wires are intended to prevent any thing from being handed to them, or from them.
And that nothing may be thrown over, and no efcapes be.
made, there is a double wall round the Lazaretto.

At the gate there is a bell to call any perfon in this en-
clofure; and by the number and other modifications of
the ftrokes, every individual knows when he is called.

The fhips are moored at the ifle of Pomeque, where a
governor refides, and other officers to keep the crews of
fhips in order, and prevent them from having any communication.* From thence goods are conveyed to the
lazarettos in large boats kept for that purpofe. Cottons
with a foul bill muft remain on the deck 7 days; and the
next 6 days, the firft bales muft remain on the bridge in
the lazaretto, before any others can be received by the porters;† after this the cargo of the fhip is brought in; but
if the fhip have a clean bill, it is unloaded much quicker,
and fubject only to twenty days quarantine: Unlefs it be
one of the two firft fhips, or there have been an account
that the plague had broke out after it had failed from the
port where it was loaded, in which cafe, it is obliged to
per-

---

* Sometimes the governor is obliged to fend fome of the French failors
to the prifon in the Lazaretto, becaufe having no pay during their quarantine, they are often quarrelfome.

† The porters are, in like manner with the guards, fent by the office,
as fhips arrive. Their number is proportioned to the cargo ; and four are
allowed to a common fhip.

perform quarantine as before faid of paffengers. And if the plague be in other cities of the Levant, five days are added to the 20 days of the quarantine: This the French call *pied de mouche*. The bales of cotton are expofed to the open air; and every ten days a feam of the bags is opened. Precious goods are placed in warehoufes with open baluftrades for the air to pafs freely.*

At Genoa, the *lazaretto* is fituated on the fea fhore, near the city, and detached from other buildings. The plan is regular; the center-row equally dividing the areas; which are 310 feet by 25. In the middle of one of the areas there is a little chapel, which has three fides open, that the elevation of the hoft may be feen in the oppofite rooms.

At the entrance there is a gaurd-room for ten foldiers, and a fpacious bake-houfe. Towards the areas are many vaulted rooms for paffengers, which open into a corridor where there are doors to feparate the paffengers of different fhips. Thefe rooms are 15 feet and 7 inches, by 14 feet 3 inches, and 11 feet and a half high. The corridor is 10 feet and 9 inches wide, and feparated from the areas by high wooden palifades. Above ftairs there are 36 rooms in front, befides 12 belonging to the prior or governor. On one fide there are 11, and on the other 10 rooms. All the rooms are nearly fimilar in length and breadth, about 16 feet nine inches, by 14 feet nine, and 11 feet fix inches high; with two oppofite windows, about 4 feet by three, and 6 feet above the floor. The windows of all the rooms are

---

* The French in every fhip have a fecretary who always performs his quarantine on fhore, and fees that none of the effects of different perfons are *mixed* or *embezzled* by the porter. He fometimes acts as doctor, and is otherwife ufeful on board. Such a fecretary I found in a *trufh* fhip.

are too fmall. The floors are brick, and the roofs vaulted. Each room has in one corner a chimney, and in
another a fewer fhut in like a clofet. Thefe rooms open
into a corridor 11 feet wide, which has fpacious windows
towards the areas, and doors which can fhut up three or
four rooms according to the number of paffengers from
each fhip. All the windows have iron bars and fhutters,
but none are glazed. Adjoining to the back of the governor's apartments is a neat and convenient chapel.
When a confiderable number are confined by ficknefs, the
chaplain refides in the governor's apartments; and then
the phyfician and furgeon are alfo obliged to refide in
their rooms, at the corner of one of the areas.

On the fecond floor there are ranges of warehoufes.
Thefe are too narrow, being only 16 feet and $\frac{1}{2}$ wide; and
the windows are too fmall, being, on one fide, only two
feet fquare; and on the other, three feet by two feet nine
inches. The floors are of ftone; but fuch floors are improper; white bricks, well burnt, being beft for goods,
becaufe lefs apt to become damp. To thefe warehoufes
there are fpacious brick afcents on the outfide, on which
bales of cotton are opened and aired. The doors are fingle; but large folding doors would have been better; and
there fhould have been a fmall partition in each of the
warehoufes, that the porters might pafs with lefs danger
of infection. The ftaircafes in the infide leading to thefe
warehoufes, and to thofe on the firft floor, are likewife too
narrow, being only 3 feet and $\frac{1}{2}$ wide.

In the centre, behind the chapel, there are two fpacious
rooms, 125 feet by 25. The afcent for bales is good,
being 10 feet wide; but the door way is only 4 feet wide.
Thefe would make good rooms for the fick; being frefh
and

and airy, and having each 20 windows, with shutters to them, and without glafs.

There are in the front three towers, or elevated rooms. That in the middle is called the governor's, becaufe it joins to his apartments. From the windows he has a full view of both the areas and corridors. But this lazaretto derives a peculiar advantage from a fine fpring of water which comes from the mountains, and contributes much to its falutarinefs. The channel is full 6 feet wide at its entrance into the area, and this renders it very convenient for wafhing linen. Being alfo properly conducted through all the fewers, it prevents the rooms from being offenfive.

There are three prifon rooms intended for riotous fail-ors who may be fent from the quarantine fhips, and for the guards and porters, fhould they happen to be diforder-ly, or guilty of embezzlement. The chief punifhment is folitary confinement, and their rooms are ill-fuited to this purpofe.*

At LEGHORN there are three *lazarettos*. One of them is new. I was there in 1788, and faw 47 flaves employed in building it. Ships which have the plague on board are now received here, and not chafed away or burnt, as is practifed in too many places. The greateft attention is given both to the health and convenience of the paffengers, and the merchandife is kept in the exacteft order. This laza-retto is called *fan Leopoldo,* in compliment to the prefent Grand Duke; and at the upper end of one of the courts is
Y placed

---

* This lazaretto has a double wall like that at *Marfeilles.* Between the walls there is a burying-ground for Proteftants, but no tomb-ftones or in-infcriptions are allowed. Here our late conful Mr *Holford* was interred. And while I was at *Genoa* a Scotch failor died in the great hofpital, who con-tinuing to the laft fteady in his religious principles, was buried here.

placed his ftatue. The repeated vifits I have paid to his prifons, hofpitals, &c. have given me the fulleft conviction that he is the true father and friend of his country.

The very worthy governor of this city *(Federigo Barbolani)* did me the favour to accompany me to this new lazaretto, and to that of fan Rocco. He alfo favoured me with the plans of three lazarettos, and with the regulations, &c. which *he* publifhed in quarto, 1785, entitled *Ordini di Sanita.* The Grand Duke, before the publication of thefe regulations, had fent a perfon to the Levant, on purpofe to gain information by returning from thence, and performing quarantine at Marfeilles, and there making the moft careful obfervations. Our ambaffador at Conftantinople (*Sir Robert Ainfley*) told me that the lazarettos at Leghorn are the beft in Europe. This was confirmed to me by two gentlemen, who had performed quarantine both there and at Marfeilles.

M A L T A.

HERE fome of the fhips from the Morca, and other places, after performing quarantine, unload their grain. At a little diftance there is a church, fituate on a high ground, and intended for the accommodations of the perfons who perform this quarantine. A letter brought by a fhip juft arrived from Turkey, was, I faw, received with a pair of iron tongs, dipped in vinegar, and then put into a cafe, and laid for a quarter of an hour on wire grates, under which ftraw and perfumes had been burnt: After which the cafe was opened, and the letter taken out by one of the directors of the office. This is the ufual method of receiving letters here.

The lazaretto at CORFU is finely fituated on a rock furrounded

rounded with water, about a league from the city. The lazaretto of CASTLE-NOVO, in Dalmatia, is on the ſhore, about two miles from the city. At the back of it there is a delightful hill, which belongs to a convent of Friars. Perſons in quarantine, after a few days, are allowed to walk there, and divert themſelves with ſhooting, &c. But, being in ſhip with a foul bill, I could not ſee any of theſe lazarettos. Their officers are dependent on the health-office at Venice, and their regulations are ſimilar.

V E N I C E.

HERE, after our ſhip had been conducted by a pilot-boat to her proper moorings, a meſſenger came from the health-office for the captain ; and I went with him in his boat, to ſee the manner in which his report was made, his letter delivered, and his examination conducted. The following morning a meſſenger came in a gondola to conduct me to the new lazaretto. I was placed, with my baggage, in a boat, faſtened by a cord ten feet long, to another boat in which were ſix rowers. When I came near the landing-place, the cord was looſed, and my boat was puſhed with a pole to the ſhore, where a perſon met me, who ſaid he had been ordered by the magiſtrates to be my guard. Soon after unloading the boat, the ſub-prior came and ſhewed me my lodgings, which was a very dirty room, full of vermin, and without table, chair, or bed. That day and the next morning I employed a perſon to waſh my room ; but this did not remove the offenſiveneſs of it, or prevent that conſtant head-ach which I had been uſed to feel in viſiting other lazarettos, and ſome of the hoſpitals in Turkey. This lazaretto is chiefly aſſigned to Turks and ſoldiers, and the crews of thoſe ſhips which have the plague on board. In one of the encloſures was the crew

of

of a Ragufian fhip, which had arrived a few days before me, after being driven from Ancona and Triefte. My guard fent a report of my health to the office, and on the reprefentation of our conful, I was conducted to the old lazaretto which is near the city. Having brought a letter to the prior from the venetian ambaffador at Conftantinople, I hoped now to have had a comfortable lodging: But I was not fo happy. The apartment appointed me (confifting of an upper and a lower room) was no lefs difagreeable and offenfive than the former. I preferred lying in the lower room on a brick floor, where I was almoft furrounded with water. After 6 days, however, the prior removed me to an apartment in fome refpects better, and confifting of four rooms. Here I had a pleafant view; but the rooms were without furniture, very ditty, and no lefs offenfive than the fick wards of the worft hofpital. The walls of my chamber, not having been cleaned probably for half a century, were faturated with infection. I got them wafhed repeatedly with boiling water, to remove the offenfive fmell, but without any effect. My appetite failed, and I concluded I was in danger of the flow hofpital fever. I propofed white wafhing my room with lime flaked in boiling water, but was oppofed by ftrong prejudice. I got, however, this one morning done through the affiftance of the Britifh conful, who was fo good as to fupply me with a quarter of a bufhel of frefh lime for the purpofe. And the confequence was, that my room was immediately rendered fo fweet and frefh, that I was able to drink tea in it in the afternoon, and to lie in it the following night. On the next day the walls were dry as well as fweet, and in a few days I recovered my appetite. Thus, at a fmall expence, and to the admiration of the other inhabitants of this lazaretto, I provided for myfelf and fucceffors, an agreeable and wholefome room, inftead of a nafty and contagious one.

Over

Over the gate-ways of two large rooms or warehoufes, were carved in ftone the images of three faints (*San Sebaf- tiano, San Marco,* and *San Rocco*) reckoned the patrons of this lazaretto. Formerly, when perfons who had the plague were brought from the city, they were put into one of thefe rooms for 40 days, and afterwards into the other for the fame time, before they were difcharged.

PAPERS RELATIVE TO THE PLAGUE.

Anfwers to Queftions concerning the Plague.

On my departure for my late tour, I was furnifhed, by two of my medical friends, *Dr Aickin* and *Dr Jebb,* with a fet of queries refpecting the plague, to be put to fome of the moft experienced practitioners in the places which I meant to vifit. I fulfilled this commiffion as well as I was able, and brought back the refult in feveral papers in the French and Italian languages, which Dr Aickin, to whofe affift- ance I am indebted for a variety of profeffional matter in this work, has methodifed and abridged fo as to form one connected article. I here give it to the public, with a view of fhewing the opinions prevalent concerning that difeafe in the countries where it is beft known by *Experi- ence,* and thereby eftablifhing fome of the moft *important facts* relative to its prevention.

I. *Is the infection of the plague frequently communicated by the touch?*

RAYMOND, *Phyfician,* MARSEILLES. It is fometimes fo communicated.

DEMOLLINS, *Surgeon,* MARSEILLES There are inftan- ces of perfons in the lazarettos who touch infected things and bodies without catching the difeafe, which is to be at- tributed to their temperament of body.

GIOVA

GIOVANELLI, *Phyfician to the lazaretto at* LEGHORN. The plague cannot be communicated without a very near approach or touch of an infected body or fubftance; and the air cannot be the vehicle of this infection.

THEY, *Phyfician to the lazaretto at* MALTA. All who approach the atmofphere of a peftilential body may receive the infection by refpiration ; and it is almoft always obferved that the contagion is received before approaching or touching the fick perfon. Yet it may happen that a perfon may inhabit the fame chamber with, and even touch a perfon in the plague without being infected ; inftances of which I have known.

MORANDI, *Phyfician,* VENICE. Contact is one of the moft powerful and dangerous means of communicating the infection ; but for the development of its effects a predifpofition in the receiving body is neceffary.

VERDONI, *Phyfician,* TRIESTE. It is moft frequently communicated by the touch, it has been given by a flower held and fmelt at, firft by two perfons who remained free, then by a third, who was feized, and died in 24 hours.

A JEW PHYSICIAN, *of* SMYRNA. The infection is in reality communicated by the touch alone; for all who keep from contact of infected perfons or things remain free. To the effect of contact, however, a certain difpofition of the air is neceffary ; for we often fee infected perfons arrive from other countries, yet the difeafe does not fpread. But what this difpofition is, can fcarcely be conceived. Commonly, in this climate, the difeafe appears at the end of fpring, and continues to the middle of fummer, with this particularity, that in cloudy weather, and

during

during the firocco wind, the attacks are more frequent. Alfo, in the fame diathefis of the air, fome receive the infection, while others, expofed to the fame danger, efcape it. From obfervation it appears, that cachectic perfons, and thofe of conftitutions abounding in acids, do not really take it. The contagious miafms may lie dormant in the body for fome time without doing the leaft harm, till fet in motion by fudden fear, or the exceffive heat of a bath.

FRA. LUIGI DI PAVIA, *Prior of the Hofpital of fan Antonia at* SMYRNA. The plague is communicated by contact, according to all the obfervations I have been able to make for eighteen years.

II. *Does the plague ever rife fpontaneoufly?*

RAYMOND. Inconteftable experience daily proves that it only proceeds from contact.

DEMOLLINS. From all ages, the plague has only been brought to Marfeilles by merchandife, or perfons from beyond fea.

GIOVANELLI. As the difeafe always appears with the fame fymptoms, it is probably not fpontaneous, but the confequence of a particular contagion.

JEW PHYSICIAN. According to the moft ancient authorities, the plague has always been brought to Smyrna by contagion, and was never produced here.

FRA. LUIGI. Ancient and common obfervation in this city proves the plague that is derived folely from contagion.

III. *To*

III. *To what distance is the air round the patient infect-ed? How far does actual contact—wearing infected clothes, or touching other things—produce the disease?*

RAYMOND. The infected are conversed with without danger across a barrier which separates them only a few paces.

DEMOLLINS. The air around the person is infected more or less according to the degree of the poison which exhales. Here, in the lazaretto, they are spoken with across two barriers a few paces from each other, without fear of contagion. Hence it would appear that the plague is communicated only by the touch, or still more by wearing infected clothes.

VERDONI. From the moment of infection, to the time when nature has entirely dissipated the contagious principle, which usually happens in 40 days, there is always a capacity of communicating infection. The degree of infection is in proportion to the volume of air surrounding the patient ; the air being what absorbs, dissipates and destroys the contagious principle. Infected substances communicate the disease for many years in proportion to the ventilation they have undergone, or of which they are susceptible.

JEW PHYSICIAN. The degree of infection in the air about the sick depends upon the greater or less malignity of the disease, and other circumstances. The air about poor patients is more infectious than about the rich. These things being established, I am of opinion, that, in the greatest contagion, one may securely see a patient at the distance of two ells (four *braccia*) if the chamber windows be not all shut.

IV.

IV. *What are the feafons in which the plague chiefly appears, and what is the interval between the infection and the difeafe?*

RAYMOND. The plague fhews itfelf at all feafons; but lefs at the two folfticcs.

DEMOLLINS. Great ravages may be made in all feafons, but principally in the great heats in fummer.

. . From the infection to the difeafe is two or three days.

GIOVANELLI. The plague appears at all times, in the fame manner as poifons at all times produce their effects. But obfervation fhews that its ravages are greater in hot feafons than in cold, and it feems that fummer and the firft months of autumn are moft to be dreaded.

There is no certainty as to the interval between the infection and the difeafe, as it depends on the particular conftitution of the patient.

THEY. Warm moift feafons contribute to the production of all contagious difeafes. The interval from the infection to the feizure is various, according to the virulence of the poifon, and conftitution of the patient. Sometimes it acts flowly, fometimes like a ftroke of lightning.

JEW PHYSICIAN. Anfwered in the firft.

FRA. LUIGI. The plague is moft fatal in Smyrna from April to July; and it is conftantly obferved that great colds and heats much diminifh it, and copious dews extinguifh it,

Z   The

The infection fhews itfelf in 24 hours, more or lefs, according to the difference of temperament.

V. *What are the* FIRST *fymptoms of the plague—are they not frequently a fwelling of the glands of the groin and armpits.*

RAYMOND. The plague often conceals itfelf under the form of an inflammatory, ardent, or malignant fever. Tumours of the glands are fometimes its firft fymptoms.

DEMOLLINS. The firft fymptoms of the plague vary; but the moft common are buboes in the armpit and groin, parotids and carbuncles in various parts of the body.

GIOVANELLI. The firft fymptoms are debility, fever, exceffive thirft followed by great heat; after which, carbuncles or buboes appear in the parotids, armpits, and groin. This laft is fooner attacked than the armpit.

FRA. LUIGI. The moft remarkable fymptoms of the plague are, turbidnefs and fparkling of the eyes, the tongue furzed with a white mucus, and very red at its tip, frequent biting of the lips, violent pain in the head, and inability to hold it up, a fenfe of great cold in the loin, vomiting, debility, fwellings of the glands are not among the firft fymptoms.

VI. *Is it true that there are two different fevers with nearly the fame fymptoms, one of which is properly termed the plague, and is communicated from a diftance by the air, and without contact; while the other, which is properly termed contagion, is only communicated by the touch, or at leaft by near approach to infected perfons or things?*

MORANDI. It is certain, from multiplied obfervations, that

that there are two forts of peftilential fevers, fimilar in appearance; one of which proceeds from the contamination of the air alone, and is communicable to any diftance; the other is produced alone by contact, or near approach. The former of thefe is properly termed a peftilential fever, the latter a contagious one.

VERDONI. The diftinction of thefe fevers is ufelefs, fince the fame which is communicated by the touch, is that alfo which is conveyed by the air to a certain diftance, efpecially in a clofe place.

JEW PHYSICIAN. That there are two kinds of plagues is abfolutely to be denied; yet fometimes it happens that perfons are attacked with the plague without knowing from whence it came.

FRA. LUIGI. I hold it for certain that there is only one fpecies of plague, though differing in malignity.

VII. *What is the method of treatment in the firft ftage— what in the more advanced periods—what is known concerning bark, fnakeroot wine, opium, pure air, the application of cold water?*

RAYMOND. The difeafe is treated as inflammatory. No fpecific has been difcovered for it.

DEMOLLINS. At the beginning—bleeding, vomiting, purgatives, diluents, refrigerants, and antifeptic are ufed; afterwards antifeptics and cordials, relatively to the temperament and fymptoms.

GIORANELLI. The plague, caufing always a difpoition to inflammation, and putrefaction, it is always proper to bleed proportionally to the strength, and to use a cooling regimen, with the vegetable acids. The repeated use of emeticks is also proper, both to cleanse the first paffages, and to dispose the virus to pass off by the skin. In the progress, it is neceffary to favour the evacuation of the virus by that issue which nature seems to point at. Thus, either antiphlogistic purgatives are to be given, if nature points that way; or suppurative plasters are to be applied to any tumours which may appear. Epispaftics to the extremities are proper where nature wants rousing. The vitriolic acid in large doses has been found very serviceable in the plague with carbuncles, as was proved in the last plague at *Mofcow*. When the inflammation is over, and marks of suppuration appear, the bark, with wine and other cordials is proper. The furgeon's affiftance is requifite in the treatment of boils and anthraxas, which last are feldom cured without the actual cautery.

They. In the beginning of pestilential fevers, bleeding is fometimes proper, and vomits almost always. In their progress, frequent fabacid and cold drinks, the bark given liberally, and vitriolic acid, have been found powerful remedies when there was a diffolution of the blood.

At Cairo they take opium, and cover themselves with mattreffes in order to excite fweat; and though parched with heat and thirft, they drink nothing. They open the immature buboes with a red hot iron.

My opinion upon the whole is, that the treatment ought to be relative to the particular conftitution of the year, and of the patient, by which the nature of the difeafe itfelf is greatly varied.

When

VIII. *When the plague prevails, do the physicians prescribe to those who have the disorder a more generous, or more abstemious diet; and do they prescribe any thing to the uninfected?*

JEW PHYSICIAN. In times of the plague, many are accustomed to eat no flesh; others, no fish; but I know not whether from the advice of physicians. For myself, I have been in many plague-years, but have made no alteration in the management of myself.

FRA. LUIGI. In Smyrna the plague is generally treated with a rigorous diet. They only use rice and vermicelli boiled in water; and sometimes, when the patient is too costive, juices and herbs boiled without any seasoning. From time to time they give some acid preserves, and raisins, and in great heats some slender lemonade, and a dish of good coffee with a biscuit every day. For drink they only use toast and water; and they follow this abstemious regimen till the fourth day of the disease is completed; after which they take chicken broth, lamb, and other food of digestion.

IX. *Are convalescents subject to repeated attacks from the same infection?*

RAYMOND. Not unless they touch something infected.

There are various opinions on this head.

X. *What is the proportion of deaths, and the usual length of the disease?*

RAYMOND. The mortality is different in different seasons and years.

DEMOL-

DEMOLLINS. In the plague at Merseilles in 1720 half the inhabitants perished. The usual length of the disease is that of other acute disorders, but longer when the tumours come to suppuration.

Sometimes it kills immediately; sometimes in 24 hours, commonly in three days. When the patient goes over the 9th day, there are great hopes of his recovery, as the buboes are not suppurated. They may, however, die within the 40th day, especially if they commit any irregularity, the principal of which is eating flesh, which instantly causes a return of fever and death. It never passes beyond the 40th day.

XI. *What are the means to prevent the plague, to stop its contagion, and to purify infected places ?*

RAYMOND. There is no other method of preserving one's-self from the plague, than avoiding the contact of infected things. Goods are purifyed by exposing them to the open air during 40 days; and furniture by a strong fumigation with aromatics and sulphur.

DEMOLLINS. Here, in the lazaretto, infected goods and furniture are exposed to a current of air for 40 days. The air of infected places is purifyed by burning all sorts of aromatic plants and sulphur.

Infected places are purifyed by fumigation and ventilation, by scraping the lime from the walls (which is then thrown into the sea) and white-washing them anew with lime and sea-water, by washing the floors, windows, doors, &c. with sea-water, then with vinegar; taking great care to leave nothing that is infected. The bodies of the dead

are

are buried in a place fet apart for that purpofe; and their beds and bedding are burned. As to other things, not ufed during the illnefs, the linen is wafhed with foap and lie; the woollen clothes are put into the fea-water for two days, and then ventilated for twenty days; thofe which would be fpoiled by water are hung on a line in the air for 40 days, and fumigated from time to time according to their quality.

VERDONI. The Greeks in Smyrna, during Lent, when they eat only vegetables, are feldom attacked; while among thofe who eat flefh the contagion makes great havock. Here the beft means of prevention are to eat moderately, and not at all of animal food; to drink water and vinegar;* to fprinkle the chamber with the latter, and ufe frequent ventilation; to change the clothes, efpecially the linen, daily, hanging in the air, from 10 to 15 days, thofe that have been ufed.

PRESERVATION FROM THE PLAGUE.

To dwell in houfes well detached from the infected, and admit no infected perfon or thing.—Habitation kept clean, and all filth removed.—Ventilation.—Windows only open while the fun is up.—Fires in each chamber, efpecially of odorous woods.—Flowers and aromatics ftrewed in the rooms.—Sprinkling with vinegar.—Fumigations with refinous and balfamic matters.

Food and drink to be ufed as found by experience to agree

* A perfon, in a very high ftation at Conftantinople, told me, that when he had the plague in that city, he lived almoft entirely on *green tea;* to which he attributed his perfect cure of that diforder: And I muft add, I have heard of fome who have made the fame ufe of brandy, and yet have recovered.

agree at other times.—Acid hubs in fallad.—Acid fruits.
—A light, brifk wine, and water, the beft for common
drink.—In fome cafes wine not to be allowed.—Purgatives
not proper without fome particular reafon for their ufe.—
Not to go out till the fun be rifen, and then not fafting.—
To avoid near approach to the infected, or touch of infected things.—The noftrils to be guarded by fnuffing up
fome odorous matter, as fp. fal. ammon. ol. fuccini, and
efpecially vinegar in a fpunge.—The mouth guarded by
chewing aromatics, as zedoary, ginger, juniper berries,
&c.—The pores of the fkin to be guarded by clothes per-
fumed with aromatics, bags worn of the fame, aromatized
unguents rubbed on various parts of the body.

The fpirits to be fupported by amufements, mirth, &c.
Effects of mufic, &c.

REMARKS on the GAOL-FEVER.

If it were afked, what is the caufe of the gaol-fever? it
would in general be readily replied, " the want of frefh
air and cleanlinefs." But as I have found, in fome prifons abroad, cells and dungeons as offenfive and dirty as
any I have obferved in this country, where, however, this
diftemper was unknown, I am obliged to look out for
fome additional caufe of its production. I am of opinion,
that the fudden change of *diet* and *lodging* fo effects the
fpirits of *new* convicts, that the general caufes of putrid
fevers exert an immediate effect upon them. Hence it is
common to fee them ficken and die in a fhort time, with
very little apparent illnefs. Convicts are generally ftout,
robuft young men, who have been accuftomed to free diet, tolerable lodgings, and vigorous excercife. Thefe are
ironed, thruft into clofe offenfive dungeons, and then chained down, fome of them without ftraw or other bedding;
here

here they continue, in winter, 16 or 17 hours out of 24, the in utter inactivity, and immersed in the noxious effluvia of their own bodies. On this account, the gaol-distemper is always observed to reign more in our prisons during winter than summer.

CONCLUSION.

In my late inquiries into the state of the *prisons* of the country, it has given me sincere pleasure to find, that, from the attention of the *magistrates*, and the operation of the salutary *Act* for preserving the health of prisoners, the gaols of the capital, though crowded, have been freed from that disease which formerly destroyed more persons than the hand of the executioner, and those in the country have been so much improved, that most of them may *now* be visited without hazard of infection; whilst the judges are secured from those risks which formerly attended them in the discharge of their *important* office. With satisfaction I have also observed the *liberal* and *humane* spirit which engaged the public to alleviate the sufferings of prisoners in general, and particularly, to release many *industrious*, though *unfortunate* debtors. But at this point, the spirit of improvement *unhappily* seems to stop, scarcely touching upon that still more *important* object, the *reformation of morals* in our prisons : Yet it is obvious that if *this* be neglected, besides the evil consequences that must result from such a source of wickedness, a suspicion will arise, that what has been already done has proceeded, *chiefly* from the selfish motive of avoiding the danger *to our own health*, in attending courts of judicature.

In this *further information*, it will be absolutely necessary to begin with the *capital* : For as, in my former visits, when I have met with the gaol-fever in county prisons, I

have

have been almoſt *conſtantly* told, that it was derived from thoſe in *London*; ſo the corruption of *manners* alſo, flowing from the great fountain, ſpreads far and wide its malignant ſtreams. In what priſon in *London* is there a proper ſeparation of criminals, the old from the young, the convicts from the untried? where are the night-rooms for ſolitary confinement and reflection? when is any proper attention paid to ſick and dying priſoners? where are the rules and orders of magiſtrates for the direction of gaolers and the government of priſoners? In what gaol are not the ears ſhocked with the *profaneneſs* of priſoners and turnkeys; When is any regard paid to the *Lord's day?* When is not the afternoon of that day a time of greater concourſe of viſitants than any other? And though the gaoler's taps are aboliſhed, yet, are not publicans *continually* waiting to ſerve the priſoners, and their company? Is not beer *now* ſold by the debtors? And do not turnkeys keep *ſhops* in the gaols?

Within 14 years, how many priſoners, together with their keepers, have I known deſtroyed by drinking, and how many convicts going out of the world in a ſtate of *intoxication!* Criminals are, for the moſt part, under the middle age of life, and therefore ſtrong enough in conſtitution to bear the trial of thoroughly breaking their bad habits; and as to debtors * who generally live in priſons in utter idleneſs, they can have little occaſion for ſtrong liquors, and would receive much more benefit from a little addition of meat and vegetables to their diet, which, by this reſtriction, they might better afford.

* Of this claſs how many perſons have I known, or heard of, who have gone into priſon *ſober* men; but who have either deſtroyed themſelves there by *drinking*, or have gone out *mere ſots?*

F   I   N   I   S.

www.ingramcontent.com/pod-product-compliance
Lightning Source LLC
Chambersburg PA
CBHW030834270326
41928CB00007B/1047